As a pastor, *The Teleios Trail* is exactly the conversation I want to have with those I serve. Bob speaks to the potential in each of us and asks the right questions to get us out of our own way to grow and abide in Christ. We may not be *teleios* yet, but this book is a phenomenal tool to spur us toward spiritual maturity.

—Dave Herndon
Church Systems Consultant
Central Kidzlink Pastor
Crossroads Community Church
Polo, IL

Finally! After 35 years of pastoral ministry, I have found a simple tool effective for helping people in their journey in discipleship. Bob Santos has a unique ability to make complex topics crystal clear and easy to understand.

—Mark Sterlace
Lead Pastor
Grace In Community Church
Alden, NY

As a pastor and Bible teacher, I found this book do three things for personal and churchwide discipleship. In each chapter, *The Teleios Trail* provokes thought and further study of areas often ignored or missed in Christian teaching. Secondly, it is a handy resource for leading new and old believers on a path to maturity in Christ. Finally, it helps answer questions to pressing issues facing the church globally with practical and scriptural insight. I recommend this book for any believer, but especially pastors and small group leaders.

—Judah Thomas
Lead Pastor
Word of Grace Fellowship
Indiana, PA

Bob Santos does a thorough job on some of the most important topics any Christian needs to grapple with in order to mature and fulfill their God-given purpose. This book will help those new to the faith see a bigger picture of how God develops purpose and it will help the more seasoned Christian gain a deeper understanding to their next step to growth.

—Kevin Bordeaux
Lead Pastor
Thrive Church
Richmond, VA

As an astute observer of both Scripture and people, Bob Santos has a unique ability to take complex subjects and make them very accessible. This book is no exception! If you desire to grow in spiritual maturity, read this book! Better yet, invite your friends, start a small group, and embark on the journey together.

—Joe Ryer
Pastor
Saving Grace Church
Indiana, PA

The Teleios Trail by Bob Santos is another valuable equipping tool from this experienced leader. Addressing a wide range of thirty important topics for spiritual growth, the book presents a tremendous starting point for developing sermons on these topics and also would serve as a valuable resource for personal or group discipleship discussions on these subjects. A wise church leader could also use it as a resource of topics to consider including in the equipping process of their church.

—Scott Dalton
International Director
Missio Global
Newark, OH

THE TELEIOS TRAIL

THIRTY TOPICS TO EXPLORE FOR SPIRITUAL GROWTH

THE TELEIOS TRAIL

THIRTY TOPICS TO EXPLORE FOR SPIRITUAL GROWTH

BOB SANTOS

SEARCH FOR ME MINISTRIES, INC.
INDIANA, PA

The Teleios Trail: Thirty Topics to Explore for Spiritual Growth
By Bob Santos

Copyright © 2024 by Search for Me Ministries, Inc.
First Edition

Cover Design and Interior Graphics: Path & Paper

Unless otherwise noted, all Scripture quotations are taken from the New American Standard Bible® (NASB1995), Copyright © 1960, 1971, 1977, 1995 by The Lockman Foundation. All rights reserved. (www.Lockman.org) Used by permission. (Old Testament prophesies quoted in the New Testament are capitalized.)

Scripture quotations marked (ESV) are from the ESV® Bible (The Holy Bible, English Standard Version®). ESV® Text Edition: 2016. Copyright © 2001 by Crossway, a publishing ministry of Good News Publishers. The ESV® text has been reproduced in cooperation with and by permission of Good News Publishers. Unauthorized reproduction of this publication is prohibited. All rights reserved.

Published by SfMe Media
Indiana, PA 15701
www.sfme.org

Printed in the United States of America

Library of Congress Control Number: 2024937239

ISBN: 978-1-937956-35-6
ePub ISBN: 978-1-937956-36-3

*To the pastors who have helped to guide and grow
me in my Christian walk*

CONTENTS

Introduction	11
Section One: Introducing Biblical Teaching	15
1. Why Spiritual Maturity Matters	17
2. Recognizing the Value of Relationships	23
3. Finding Wisdom in the Word	29
4. Fearing the Lord	35
5. Presenting Relevant Messages	43
6. Starting at the Beginning	49
Section Two: Discerning the Way Forward	53
7. Investigating Humanity's Crash	55
8. Discerning Law and Grace	61
9. Knowing Why Faith Matters	67
10. Fulfilling the Greatest Commandment	73
11. Embracing the Essence of Christian Living	79
12. The Reality of Judgment from on High	85
Section Three: Growing in Faith	95
13. Welcoming the King's Domain	97
14. Overcoming Hindrances to Prayer	103
15. Honoring the Covenants	109
16. Establishing a Secure Identity	115
17. Pulling Down Idols	121
18. Severing the Evil Root	127

Section Four: Solidifying the Distinctives of Maturity — 133

19. Preserving the Unity of the Faith — 135
20. Learning to Resolve Conflict Well — 141
21. Dealing with Counterfeit Leaders — 147
22. Caring for Ourselves — 155
23. Glorifying God — 161
24. Cultivating Faithfulness — 169

Section Five: Making a Difference — 175

25. Walking in Freedom — 177
26. Navigating Our Era — 187
27. Living with Purpose — 193
28. Empowering People for Change — 199
29. Redefining Success — 207
30. Persevering through Adversity — 213

INTRODUCTION

Service to God and humanity often begins with a burden. After losing a son to an overdose, a man might launch a drug-alcohol rehabilitation ministry. A woman, heartbroken at the sight of orphaned children, takes the bold step of opening an orphanage. In a multitude of scenarios, people burdened by poverty, brokenness, and loss feel compelled to do something about those issues. And so they set out to facilitate change.

I carry a burden too. I can trace its roots to when I became a Christian and got involved with a vibrant campus fellowship. "We can make a difference!" our weekly speakers exhorted. And I believed them.

Recognizing that the church is God's primary vehicle for advancing His purposes on earth, I immersed myself in congregational life not long after graduation. My heart soon sank in disappointment, though. A vast gulf seemed to separate my idealized vision of the church and the reality I was now facing. Becoming a board member opened my eyes even more to the underbelly of local church life. Sadly, a large number of people who had virtually grown up in the church displayed their spiritual immaturity by both word and deed.

Imagine asking a group of regular church attenders about God's intended purpose for pastoral ministry. How do you think they would respond? Most would say God gives pastors the responsibility of caring for His sheep. Others might highlight the need to preach the gospel for salvation, or to teach people how to live out the basic principles of the Bible. A handful might even mention equipping God's people for the work of the ministry.

I would not argue against any of these answers, but I would add yet another response—one that is implicit to some but hardly considered by others. *God calls pastors and other ministry leaders to spur people's growth toward spiritual maturity.* According to the apostle Paul:

> We proclaim Him, admonishing every man and teaching every man with all wisdom, so that we may present every man complete in Christ. For this purpose also I labor, striving according to His power, which mightily works within me. Colossians 1:28–29

A devoted Christian might fixate on the quest to live a flawless life, but that is not the mindset communicated by Scripture. The Greek word translated as "complete" in this passage is *teleios*. A primary meaning connotes "having reached its utmost development"[1]—as in an adult growing to full maturity.

We strive not to produce flawless Christians, but maturing ones. Perfect people are mythological creatures, existing only in the human imagination. In reality, we seek to facilitate a *growth process* that propels spiritual children into adulthood.

Now, imagine asking our same group of churchgoers why *they* attend? Again, the responses would vary. Some value the relationships. Others might feel the need to check off items on a list intended to gain God's approval. But how many would identify *the need to grow* as a core motivation?

We often encounter a disconnect between what church leaders expect, what church attenders expect, and what God expects. And while most pastors believe they are doing their best to help people become all the Lord intends, an honest survey of the Western church will show considerable room for improvement.

Yes, some pastors have abandoned God's plan, but even devoted clergy face steep challenges. Pastoral responsibilities can be overwhelming. The Western family is coming apart at the seams. And modern technology has created an onslaught of

---

[1]. Alexander Souter, *A Pocket Lexicon to the Greek New Testament* (Oxford: Clarendon Press, 1917), 258.

temptations and distractions. These—and other issues—combine to make spiritual maturity all the more elusive.

I am not saying the situation is beyond hope, but our approach most certainly needs to be adjusted. Many church growth efforts focus on quantitative issues addressed through styles, techniques, and systems. And while a need for this approach exists, numerical growth without depth will always leave us wanting. The church of Jesus Christ is much too important for us to be content with shallow faith.

How do people grow to spiritual maturity? The incorruptible seed of God's Word, as it bears fruit in human hearts, must always be central to the process. I am not referring to His Word as a vehicle of behavior modification, but as the source of *internal transformation*.

We often find it easier, however, to use the Christian Bible as a tool for behavior modification than as a source of spiritual transformation. Telling people how to live can be easy; helping them renew their minds presents a far greater challenge. Human nature is tricky, and the breadth of knowledge found within the many pages of Scripture can leave us wondering where to begin. Even seasoned pastors will struggle deciding what topics to address. In this, *The Teleios Trail* should prove quite useful.

Through four-plus decades of helping nurture both young and old toward spiritual growth, I have identified key Biblical themes that help facilitate the process. Some of these themes remain highly regarded, and thus widely taught; others receive little attention. But in all honesty, my goal in penning these pages is not so much to teach as to *spur thought*. I hope to stimulate the thinking of people who help others grow.

The primary intent of this book is to provide a resource for pastors, small group leaders, campus ministers, and any others involved with the painstaking work of growing people. And though I desire to help spur and equip leaders, I also want to stimulate the thinking of people who are seeking to grow. They, too, can benefit richly from the concepts presented.

The Teleios Trail introduces topics I have found useful—if not necessary—for helping Christians grow to maturity. The information regarding each topic is not comprehensive, and neither is the list of topics itself. Limitations of time, space, and personal understanding prevent me from doing more. Still, the reader can glean much from a book such as this.

After presenting a topic related to spiritual growth, each chapter is followed by multiple questions related to that topic. Depending on your motivation for reading, you can:

- compile messages for preaching or teaching.
- decide what to cover for discipleship training.
- meet with a small study group to discuss the topics.
- create a personal growth plan of topics to further enhance your own walk with God.

Regardless of the reason you choose to embark on *The Teleios Trail*, I pray that it sparks an exciting process of discovery and growth!

Section One

Introducing Biblical Teaching

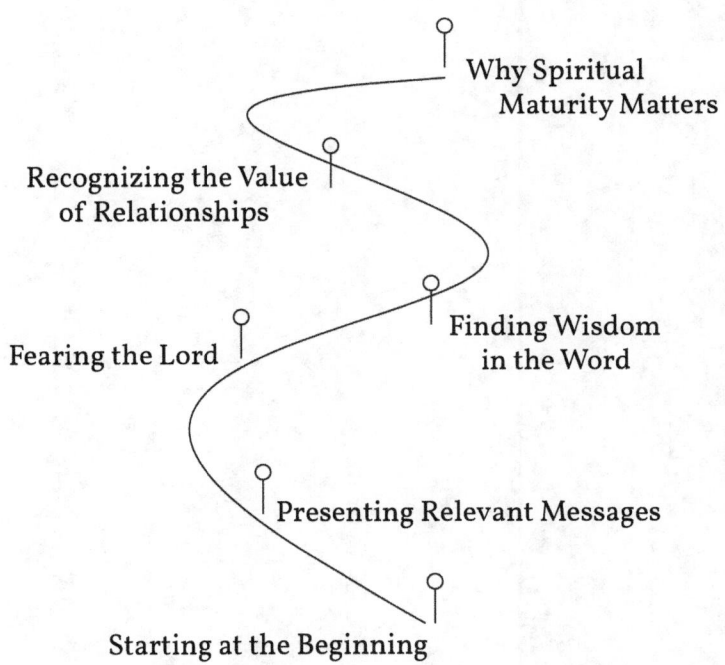

- Why Spiritual Maturity Matters
- Recognizing the Value of Relationships
- Finding Wisdom in the Word
- Fearing the Lord
- Presenting Relevant Messages
- Starting at the Beginning

We proclaim Him, admonishing every man and teaching every man with all wisdom, so that we may present every man complete in Christ. For this purpose also I labor, striving according to His power, which mightily works within me.

Colossians 1:28–29

CHAPTER ONE

WHY SPIRITUAL MATURITY MATTERS

I became a Christian while in college, thanks in part to the efforts of students involved with an active and vibrant campus ministry. Growth came quickly in that dynamic environment, birthing within me a new vision for life. We were going to help change the world, and so my wife Debi and I joined a local church not long after graduating.

It was not much longer until I found myself sitting at a table with fellow church board members. All kinds of insecure thoughts flooded my mind. How could I, as a twenty-five-year-old, be qualified to sit with seasoned, gray-haired elders?

My nervousness was not all negative. Being given a voice as a church leader also excited me. Convinced that the church is God's primary vehicle for touching our world, my heart celebrated the opportunity to make a difference. Reality set in quickly.

About six years later, as my second term on the board neared its end, I decided it was time for a new direction. While I had learned much, and we had accomplished some good things, the overall experience left me feeling disappointed. Dozens of pin pricks had deflated my once-lofty opinion of the church.

The lack of spiritual maturity stood out most. People who had been members for thirty, forty, and even fifty years were still acting like spiritual babies. Instead of making significant forward progress in advancing God's kingdom, we had spent far too many hours trying to soothe and pacify fully grown children.

I can recall some bright spots in that early leadership experience, but the negative encounters with people who identified as "God's family" marked me forever. As much as I believe in the importance of evangelism and bringing the lost into the fold, I have also learned that spiritual immaturity undermines our ability to fulfill the Great Commission. When professing Christians display self-centered and immature behavior, unbelievers recoil in disgust. If we focus on reaching the lost without making mature disciples, the fruit of our own labors can significantly hinder our God-given mission.

DEFINING SPIRITUAL MATURITY

Pastors readily recognize the difficulties of dealing with spiritually immature people, but we also struggle to define such a broad concept. A 2009 study by the Barna Group revealed some of the confusion involved:

> One of the widely embraced notions about spiritual health is that it means "trying hard to follow the rules described in the Bible" – 81% of self-identified Christians endorsed this statement, and a majority agreed strongly (53%). Even among those individuals defined by their belief that salvation is not earned through "good works," four out of five born again Christians concurred that spiritual maturity is "trying hard to follow the rules."[1]

When I first read this article, I had difficulty believing it to be true. If we understand the dynamics of the gospel of grace, we will realize that "trying hard to follow the rules" will put us on a path to *immaturity*. Today, our collective cluelessness regarding spiritual maturity seems even more pronounced.

---

1. "Many Churchgoers and Faith Leaders Struggle to Define Spiritual Maturity," Barna Group, May 11, 2009, accessed January 25, 2024, https://www.barna.com/research/many-churchgoers-and-faith-leaders-struggle-to-define-spiritual-maturity/.

If it is not about trying to follow the rules, what does spiritual maturity involve? And how do we get there? Let us begin by identifying several marks of a spiritually mature person:

- A self-starter
- Humble
- Motivated by love
- Graceful through adversity
- Discerning
- Persevering

A SELF-STARTER

Children are naturally immature. Only after much prodding and discipline will the average child fulfill personal responsibilities such as cleaning up toys. We do not need to remind spiritually mature Christians about the importance of daily devotions, commitment to learning, or service to God. They innately understand these things are integral to Christian living, and so they take personal initiative to make them happen.

HUMBLE

Jesus, of course, is our prime example of humility. Though He came as God in human flesh, the self-proclaimed "Son of Man" never elevated Himself in a prideful way. Nor did He live as though everything was about Him. Instead, the Son of God was so secure in His identity that He lowered Himself to serve others.

MOTIVATED BY LOVE

The roots of Christian living stem from a heart of love, whatever form that love might take. And being other-centered goes hand in hand with humility. In contrast, spiritual immaturity is all about

ME—MY needs and *MY* desires. Such self-centered thinking fuels a consumer mindset in the local church—with devastating effects. Lesser issues demand attention, material resources go toward unfruitful projects, and unnecessary conflicts drain human energy. These all combine to compromise the church's life-giving mission.

Selfish people also look for angles to exploit as they tear down others for personal benefit. But in God's dynamic, whether by word or action, love calls us to build others up. We can identify spiritually mature believers by their edifying mindsets that seek to add value to others. Real love gives and edifies.

GRACEFUL THROUGH ADVERSITY

On this planet, *everyone* faces adversity. We all experience times of hardship, loss, and betrayal. Even when in pain, a spiritually mature person will seek to avoid unnecessary drama. Being grounded in faith and love, he or she will follow a path of wisdom over emotion.

DISCERNING

Immature people are especially susceptible to the influences of human opinions and deceptive doctrines. Mature believers, however, will learn discernment by cultivating sensitivity to the Holy Spirit, along with an in-depth understanding of God's Word. Facts and information have their place, but understanding the dynamics of truth enables us to identify false doctrines and deadly traps.

PERSEVERING

Growing to spiritual maturity involves a long, fluid process. It does not happen in a day, or even a year. Nor can we always identify a person's level of maturity by a snapshot. Maturity is the product of persistent forward movement through the peaks and valleys of life.

WHY SPIRITUAL MATURITY MATTERS

My list is by no means exhaustive, and perhaps you have something to add. What matters most, however, is the *fruit*. If people are not growing toward maturity, a church will become inwardly focused even while trying to accomplish its outward purposes.

A nonstop parade of drama and complaints will steal our focus and consume precious resources of time, energy, and money. Everyone has issues and struggles in life, but the key question involves whether we are growing in God's grace through those struggles. If our people do not grow to maturity, they will steal our attention at the expense of our mission. This matters because eternal destinies are at stake.

Immaturity also leads to a "revolving door" in the church. Young people, provoked by hypocrisy, will become disenchanted and move away from church and faith. Meanwhile, many who are more grounded in the faith will quietly transition to healthier congregations.

Make no mistake; the vitality of church life and effectively fulfilling our mission depend upon God's people growing to spiritual maturity!

THE BOTTOM LINE

Effectively advancing God's kingdom on earth requires devoted believers who are growing toward spiritual maturity. If people are not growing, a church will focus inward—either by choice or by the need to deal with unnecessary drama. Only as the members of Christ's body mature can a church gain lasting momentum in its efforts to reach the world and advance God's purposes on our fallen planet.

RELEVANT QUESTIONS

1. Can you recall any frustrating situations you have encountered with spiritual immaturity? Please be discreet with names and places.
2. How do you see spiritual immaturity hindering the Great Commission?
3. Talk through the marks of spiritual maturity:
    a. A self-starter
    b. Humble
    c. Motivated by love
    d. Graceful through adversity
    e. Discerning
    f. Persevering
4. What would you add to this list?
5. How do you think seasoned Christians respond when spiritual immaturity becomes the norm in a church?
6. What is your organization's vision to help people grow toward spiritual maturity?

CHAPTER TWO

RECOGNIZING THE VALUE OF RELATIONSHIPS

For as long as I have been a Christian, the desire to understand and expound upon Biblical principles has burned in my heart. Knowing God's truth and experiencing the resulting freedom does not come simply from accumulating knowledge about God and the Bible, but from a deep, intimate understanding of the Lord and His design for humanity. And because everything about the Christian faith centers on a relationship with our Creator, the learning process can never be entirely academic.

For some people, religious practice involves accumulating knowledge, following prescribed rituals, and doing good deeds—all while serving God from afar. But this approach misses the heart of His good plan. *What matters most—always—is our relationship with the Lord.*

From the beginning of time, the King of Glory created humans for a unique relationship with Him. The Christian Scriptures regard that relationship as the ultimate goal. Think of Abraham, Moses, and the people of Israel. Think of Jesus coming to earth, training disciples, and living among the people. Think about the Holy Spirit being poured out on the Day of Pentecost. And think of heaven and God's people spending eternity in His presence.

Christians are to be set apart from the commonality and corruption of this world to enjoy an intimate and abiding relationship with the God who created us. This involves a lifelong process of learning His ways, aligning our lives with His design, and being conformed to His image. The heavenly Father takes great interest in this growth process—often called "sanctification"—as He seeks to transform our lives.

Integral to God's good design, we also see the importance of *growing together*. Is this not a primary foundation of local church ministry? We seek, serve, and worship the Lord together. Some people attempt to walk with God apart from local church involvement. But those efforts fall far short of their potential, making spiritual maturity no more than a fleeting dream.

The importance of relationships begins with the Trinity. Three Persons form a *single* entity. The mystery is deep, but it proclaims a clear and universal message: *our God is relational*. And being created in His image, we are relational too. Having lived in the realm of isolation more than I have wanted, I can say that virtually every aspect of life proves more difficult without vital relationships. Yes, our interpersonal connections are imperfect and carry their own challenges, but they also bless us in untold ways.

QUESTIONS AND DIALOGUE

Truly effective learning depends upon relational environments. Regardless of the social or academic sphere involved, education requires an opportunity to ask questions and discuss ideas. How much more does this apply to grasping Biblical concepts? Spiritual growth involves laying hold of the mysteries of God, but there is a reason they are called "mysteries." Understanding God's ways does not come easily or naturally, which is why we all need opportunities to ask questions in nonjudgmental settings.

The quip "Don't ask questions; just believe it!" does nothing to help people grow. Such statements do more damage than good. Inquisitive minds will always bring questions to the table, which helps foster growth. But if not adequately addressed, those inquiries can also foster doubts about God and His goodness.

The attitude with which we respond to genuine, meaningful questions will breed either life or death.

Jesus once told a group of believing Jews, "If you continue in My word, then you are truly disciples of Mine; and you will know the truth, and the truth will make you free" (John 8:31b–32). Knowing the truth is not just about possessing a set of facts pertaining to God; it also includes developing an *intimate understanding* of His ways. And when people begin to understand the profound wisdom behind Christianity, their faith blossoms. But if vital questions go unanswered, doubts about God's goodness will likely fester and create spiritual decay.

We cannot answer every question about God, but we can bring them into the light by facilitating discussion in nonjudgmental environments. This approach might create some uncomfortable moments, but that is far better than allowing sincere questions to turn into festering doubts amid the darkness of isolation. Even when we do not have adequate answers, we can still support and encourage people as they wrestle with their doubts. Otherwise, they might find listening ears among enemies of the gospel who hijack honest questions for ungodly purposes.

To take these ideas a step further, it has been my experience that people—even Christian leaders—are generally poor listeners. As we dialogue with others, we tend to "keep our answers running." What I mean is that, rather than truly listening, our thoughts focus on how to respond. This tendency is especially pronounced when topics are controversial and emotions heightened. Most people know whether they are being heard, and if we fail to listen well, they will take it as a sign of disrespect. We will then lose them in the conversation regardless of how good our arguments might be.

GOD'S RELATIONAL DESIGN

During His time on earth, our Lord trained a group of disciples to advance His kingdom. These men walked with Jesus, asked hard questions, and watched Him navigate the challenges of life and ministry. The crowds followed Jesus and received His touch, but Christ's disciples were the ones who grew to maturity. To truly grow, people need models—and not just from a distance. In this regard, healthy relationships are vital.

Walking with God is no minor endeavor. Choosing to surrender one's life to Christ creates a seismic upheaval of what we naturally think, say, and do. Such a decision also compels us to swim against the cultural tide. Only together as the body of Christ can we face such heavy-duty challenges, drawing comfort, strength, and wisdom from one another during times of adversity and need.

According to the apostle Paul, the growth process also involves "speaking the truth in love" (Ephesians 4:15), and bringing gentle correction when necessary (Galatians 6:1). We are all prone to selfish and deceptive thinking, but healthy relationships challenge us to address our issues and stay true to the faith.

THE MIND OF CHRIST

"We have the mind of Christ," Paul wrote to the church in Corinth (1 Corinthians 2:16). This statement has always intrigued me. To have the mind of the God who created *everything* is amazing!

Let us be honest; no one person or organization has it all. While it is natural for us to think that we have exclusive access to God's truth, reality tells a different story. Yes, the Holy Spirit dwells within us as believers, but the mind of Christ is far too large for any one person or organization. To gain the mind of Christ in its fullness, we need humble dialogue through which we learn from one another.

Throughout the course of my life, I have taught many a Sunday school class and led many a small group. And though I am often the primary teacher, my understanding of God always increases through our group dialogue. No one person has it all, and fully knowing the mind of Christ requires a relational, collective element.

SHARPENING ONE ANOTHER

Because people are imperfect, relationships can be messy and uncomfortable. But that, too, is part of the growing process. Ultimately, we are helping people grow in love, which requires opportunities for hearts to be tested and stretched.

Like many of you, I have experienced difficulties in local churches that should have never happened. While not outright abusive, those situations hurt me deeply. Each time, I had to choose between honoring my Savior with humble love, or elevating self and growing bitter. Those cumulative choices had a maturing effect on me. Love will not always come easily, but through our relational challenges, we will grow.

We cannot identify a single type of relational environment that works best for everyone. Small group meetings, Sunday School classes, and one-on-one discipleship meetings can all foster growth when characterized by love and humility.

One truth remains, however: while sermons play a vital role, they cannot stand alone. Very few church services provide the type of relational environment necessary to maximize growth. Thus, the maturing process can never depend entirely on a pastor. We also need key leaders to guide discussion, model truth, and bring correction when needed. *We are all in this together, and only together can we grow to our full potential.*

THE BOTTOM LINE

Combining the ideas of this chapter, we can gain considerable insight into God's purposes for His church, which is the body of Christ (Ephesians 1:22–23). And how we need such a perspective in a world where people feel they can walk with God while avoiding His body!

Yes, we can speak of the church universal—of which all genuine Christians are members. But the New Testament assumes we will also connect with a local expression of Christ's body. Local churches are not perfect by any means, and some are healthier than others. But we are all members of one another, and together, we edify and build one another up.

Those who want to walk with God and grow to maturity must involve themselves locally. And those who lead local fellowships should work to create environments in which healthy relationships flourish.

RELEVANT QUESTIONS

1. What do you think of the idea that God is a relational Being?
2. Why is it vital that people be able to ask honest questions?
3. How can we create an environment that fosters meaningful dialogue?
4. What is the advantage of allowing people to bring their doubts into the light?
5. How does the attitude with which we respond to genuine questions breed either life or death?
6. What does it mean to "speak the truth in love"?
7. What is the difference between having an intimate understanding of God's truth as opposed to merely accumulating knowledge about God?
8. Are you actively involved with a local expression of Christ's body? Why or why not?
9. What relational opportunities does your church provide for growth? Are there others that can be added to the mix?
10. How can relational conflicts contribute to the maturing process?

CHAPTER THREE

FINDING WISDOM IN THE WORD

No person can mature spiritually apart from the Bible. Human reasoning has led to many discoveries, but never an understanding of God's ways. And if His Word is not integral to the growth process, any effort regarding spirituality will lead to deception.

Quoting Deuteronomy 8:3, our Lord once proclaimed, "Man shall not live by bread alone, but by every word that comes from the mouth of God" (Matthew 4:4, ESV). Growing to spiritual maturity does not happen without spiritual nourishment, and such nourishment does not exist apart from the Bible—the living Word of God.

I have never conducted a survey on the matter, but I would guess most pastors profess to "preach the Word of God." What it means to preach the Word, however, can be a matter of debate. Central to the issue is the *authority* of the Bible. Anyone can use the Bible as a text, but spiritual transformation requires embracing it as our *standard* for spiritual truth. In this, we can identify three primary statements regarding the Christian Scriptures:

1. **God *inspired* the writing of the Bible.** When heaven breathes, earth lives. Because the Word proceeds from the mouth of God, it is *inspired* by our Creator (2 Timothy 3:16). We are not just talking about words on a page, or even good ideas, but about the *living Word* infused with the breath of God. And because the Word is alive, it also has the power to transform.

2. **The Bible is *infallible*.** People often struggle to trust the Bible. It was penned in ancient times, and the process of transmission required the painstaking work of human copyists. We do not have screenshots or computer drives with copies of the originals, and so it is reasonable that people would have questions. Thankfully, archaeology, history, and textual studies have produced abundant evidence to support the integrity of this amazing book.

   When we say that the Bible is infallible, we mean it is always correct regarding spiritual matters. Thus, it will *never fail* to accomplish the purposes for which God sent it (Isaiah 55:11). Our spiritual growth is central to His purposes, and that growth sprouts from confidence in the truth of His Word.

3. **The Bible serves as our *authority* for spiritual truth.** In modern culture, conflict rages around the Bible's authority over human lives. It is one thing to use the Bible as a helpful or inspirational text, and another to declare it as the *authoritative standard* for spiritual truth. Because God is sovereign over the universe, His Word carries the highest authority in language and communication (John 17:17). If we fail to esteem the Bible as such, we open the door for deceptive ideas to wreak havoc.

LITERAL OR FIGURATIVE?

I once took a Christianity class at a secular university. What an interesting experience that was! Early in the course, our professor asked a provoking question: "Should the Bible be taken literally or figuratively?" My answer was an unequivocal "Yes!" Much—but not all—of Scripture is presented as literal truth, making his question a false dichotomy.

The Bible itself says that Jesus used *figures of speech* (John 10:6), and scholars tell us they are interspersed throughout the Scriptures. This issue brings us to one of our most formidable challenges involved with understanding the Bible: how do we know what to accept as literal truth and what to take figuratively?

A second question follows closely: Should God have made everything so clear as to eliminate any possibility of confusion?

If the Scriptures simply provided a guide for moral living, complete clarity would indeed be warranted. But the Bible is something more than a moral handbook. It is a book of *relationship*, and the process of unpacking its truths requires drawing near to its Author. Wisdom from heaven is what we need, and thankfully, the Lord wants us to know and understand His ways. Doing so, however, is more an issue of the heart than the mind.

THE PATH TO WISDOM

We all naturally elevate our personal perspectives (i.e., our own wisdom) above others. I grew up in a blue-collar community with no shortage of farms, and I also spent multiple decades relating to university academics. Both groups routinely belittle the other for their inability to see clearly. Regardless of educational level, viewing one's personal perspective as the standard for truth represents the norm. My opinion is always right because, well, it is *my* opinion.

A multitude of problems result from our arrogance. And if we consider the innumerable conflicts and pervasive divisions in our society, much of it traces back to intellectual pride. Arrogance of the mind never serves us well—especially in a relationship with God. Isaiah 55 proclaims that His ways are on a *higher plane*, entirely different from our own.

> Seek the Lord while He may be found;
> Call upon Him while He is near.
> Let the wicked forsake his way
> And the unrighteous man his thoughts;
> And let him return to the Lord,
> And He will have compassion on him,
> And to our God,

> For He will abundantly pardon.
> "For My thoughts are not your thoughts,
> Nor are your ways My ways," declares the Lord.
> "For as the heavens are higher than the earth,
> So are My ways higher than your ways
> And My thoughts than your thoughts."
> Isaiah 55:6–9

The distance mentioned in this passage is primarily of *contrast*. God's thinking is on an entirely different plane than ours, and those who think naturally will *never* align with our Creator's wise design. The path to wisdom requires that we humble our pride and admit our inability to see spiritual matters clearly.[1]

THE MISSING ELEMENT

How many Christians recognize the vast gulf between human wisdom and divine? And just as importantly, how many actively seek God for an understanding of His ways? The Bible admonishes us to look to the Lord for wisdom—even to the point of pursuing it as we would *hidden treasure* (Proverbs 2:4). How many of us take that admonition seriously?

Can you imagine what would happen if word got out that a wealthy merchant buried a chest of gold bars in your local park? Chaos would erupt, with treasure seekers overturning every blade of grass in their quest for material wealth. When we clamor for money but yawn at God's wisdom, it is no wonder we remain blind.

From what I have seen, it is rare for Christians to pray for wisdom, let alone to do so fervently. This effort to seek is the element of change we so often miss. And it shows by the foolish decisions we so often make. If we want our people to grow to spiritual maturity, we must coach them to fervently petition the Savior to open their eyes to His ways.

---

1. My book *Say Goodbye to Regret: Discovering the Secret to a Blessed Life* provides a more comprehensive look at this vital topic of wisdom.

THE DANGERS OF A HARDENED HEART

Humanity has another common problem that hinders our grasp of divine wisdom: hardened hearts. In Ephesians 4:17-19, the apostle Paul wrote of Gentiles who were darkened in their understanding and alienated from the life of God because of their hardness of heart. Unfortunately, unbelievers are not the only ones affected. Even Jesus' disciples failed to see the Son of God clearly, and He alluded to hardened hearts as a cause for their blindness (Mark 8:17-18).

Christians today face an almost overwhelming temptation to become hardened. American culture is jettisoning Biblical principles at an alarming rate, and enemies of the gospel are using unjust tactics to make it happen. This is especially true in the political realm. And while we want to exert a godly influence on the world of government, we dare not allow ourselves to be drawn into the political vortex of harsh, belittling, and abrasive rhetoric. Fanning the flames of rage might get people to donate money or vote for a particular cause, but even a low-grade simmering anger will blind them to the light of God's wisdom.

The writer of Proverbs admonishes the reader to "watch over your heart with all diligence, for from it flow the springs of life" (Proverbs 4:23). In our context, this means loving our enemies (Matthew 5:43-44), and choosing to forgive those who hurt us (Colossians 3:13). How uncommon this approach has proven to be—even in Bible-rich environments!

Not only does unconditional love set Christianity apart from other religions, its effect upon the human heart also opens the gateway to divine wisdom. If we want to see into God's mind, we must do so according to His heart.

Finally, as a word of caution, compassion and wisdom should always go hand in hand. Yes, we want to soften our hearts and care deeply about others. But those who exercise compassion apart from wisdom will open the door for lawlessness and chaos, wasting valuable resources in the process.

THE BOTTOM LINE

The Bible is humanity's inspired, infallible, and authoritative standard for spiritual truth. If we want to favorably influence others, we will humble our hearts and cry out for wisdom to divide properly the living Word of God. We will also encourage our people to seek the Lord's wisdom for themselves.

Spiritual growth begins with understanding and aligning with God's ways, and that is not something we could ever do by following our natural thought processes. Instead, we must humble our hearts, let go of anger and bitterness, and actively seek our Creator for wisdom. This simple pattern will then set the stage to welcome His kingdom life into our midst.

RELEVANT QUESTIONS

1. What does it mean to you that the Bible is inspired by God?
2. How does the authoritative nature of the Bible play into our discipleship efforts?
3. How does intellectual pride hinder spiritual growth?
4. What is Isaiah 55:6–9 communicating?
5. How does a hardened heart hinder us from understanding the Lord's ways?
6. What factors contribute to hearts becoming hard?
7. What steps can we take to soften our hearts to better receive God's wisdom?
8. How can we help soften others so they are more open to His truth?
9. How often do you cry out for God's wisdom? In what ways can you improve in this area?
10. What happens when we have compassion without wisdom?

CHAPTER FOUR

FEARING THE LORD

Most of us have grown up using *idioms* to describe our experiences in life. For example, if my friends and I were playing baseball and one of them hit a drive just beyond the foul line, he might exclaim, "That was so close!" In response, another friend would quip, "Close only counts in horseshoes and hand grenades!" The hand grenade reference is obvious. And for those unfamiliar with the game of horseshoes, a player can score points just by getting close to the stake.

There are many areas of life in which close is not good enough. Almost enough money will not buy a meal. Nor will almost enough gas get you to your destination. Can you imagine a bride's reaction if her groom almost made it to the wedding on time?

THEOLOGICAL NEAR MISSES

Regarding Biblical truth, the Western church is plagued by what I call "theological near misses." These are important areas of doctrine in which we might be mostly right, but with just enough missing or wrong to throw us off track. With some issues, a near miss might not matter much. But with others, the implications can be enormous.

We know that only a minor error in navigation at the beginning of a flight can have profound implications by the end. Similarly, instead of producing devoted disciples of Christ, "close but not quite" theology related to the gospel has created a consumer mindset within many churches. The church, people begin to think, exists to meet their needs and fulfill their desires. How does this happen? All too easily!

The Bible is not an easy book to navigate. Not only do we find its pages long and content rich, but we also encounter significant challenges in seeking to understand God's intent. For example, if we read the story about the woman caught in adultery (John 8:3–11), we might struggle to reconcile Jesus' response with the old covenant command condemning adultery (Leviticus 20:10).

Public perceptions of Biblical truth can also shift over time. Academic instruction and pastoral preaching, along with the spiritual music of the age, all influence these perceptions. I am not suggesting that we discount influential scholars, pastors, and songwriters, but that we build unbiased belief systems on the timeless truths of God's Word.

More than what influential Pastor A or B is preaching, we should ask, "What is God's reality?" Accurately answering that question requires honest and objective study of the Scriptures that is rooted in heavenly wisdom.

FEARING GOD

Throughout this book, I address several theological near misses in a quest to help us better discern Biblical truth. But early on, I want to present a topic the global church has struggled with throughout the years: the fear of the Lord.

We read stories in the Old Testament about people trembling in fear at the manifestation of God's presence. One of the most significant, recorded by the pen of Moses, took place on Mount Sinai just before God handed down the Ten Commandments:

> So it came about on the third day, when it was morning, that there were thunder and lightning flashes and

a thick cloud upon the mountain and a very loud trumpet sound, so that all the people who were in the camp trembled. And Moses brought the people out of the camp to meet God, and they stood at the foot of the mountain.

Now Mount Sinai was all in smoke because the Lord descended upon it in fire; and its smoke ascended like the smoke of a furnace, and the whole mountain quaked violently. When the sound of the trumpet grew louder and louder, Moses spoke and God answered him with thunder. Exodus 19:16–19

Understandably, this close encounter with God struck terror in human hearts.

Have you ever experienced the raw forces of nature? An exploding volcano, for example, might leave a person breathless. And though few of us have encountered anything so extreme, we have at least gotten hints of what nature can do. Many more have suffered pain and loss.

I enjoy being on the water. Whether it be a small mountain stream or a vast ocean, the mere presence of nature's water refreshes my soul like nothing else. One summer afternoon, my adult kids and I went whitewater rafting in the mountains of North Carolina. Paddling in pairs in small "ducky" boats on the scenic Nantahala River, we darted in and out of rapids and around rocks. All went well until the last class III rapid. I am still not sure how it happened, but my daughter Beth and I flipped the ducky and spilled into the raging water. Its power caught me by surprise.

I like to fish for trout, so I have waded rivers before, but always in places of my choosing. On that day, I felt powerless against the force of the flow. Thankfully, the river opened into a large pool, so Beth and I were able to work our way to the edge of the water. From there, others easily pulled us to safety.

HUMAN PERSPECTIVES

My experience on the Nantahala involved only a small river on a planet with a 24,900-mile circumference. And that planet revolves around an average-sized star resting in a single galaxy. We cannot even begin to fathom the breadth of our universe, and yet the Lord simply *spoke* it all into existence with a handful of words. If we add the intensity of God's holiness into the mix, we recognize the Almighty to be truly fearsome. Strangely, though, He does not want us to be terrified of His presence.

For many centuries, Christian preaching was law-based, emphasizing judgment (more on that later) and the severe consequences of a life apart from God. Even seasoned believers lived in near-constant fear of losing their salvation. Many souls were repulsed by the constant drumbeat of anger and wrath.

In more recent years, Christian preaching and teaching have revealed the grace of God like never before. Finally, people began to grasp the depths of the Lord's love, along with His deep desire to be near His human creations. Unfortunately, much of Western church culture has also lost a healthy fear—*reverence* is probably a better word—of the Lord. An oversimplified message of grace (more on that later too), combined with a cultural lack of respect for authority, has led many to view God as a permissive parent who routinely fails to follow through on promised consequences for wrongdoing.

A NEW TESTAMENT PERSPECTIVE

Having a healthy fear of God is more than just a concept from the Old Testament (1 Peter 2:17). Our Creator is all-powerful and awesome—awe-inducing, in the truest sense of the word. A deep sense of reverence will always be due His name.

The apostle John enjoyed being one of Jesus' closest companions when He walked this earth. It was John who leaned against Jesus' breast during the Last Supper. But the Book of

FEARING THE LORD

Revelation records a much different kind of encounter between John and the Son of God.

> Then I turned to see the voice that was speaking with me. And having turned I saw seven golden lampstands; and in the middle of the lampstands I saw one like a son of man, clothed in a robe reaching to the feet, and girded across His chest with a golden sash. His head and His hair were white like white wool, like snow; and His eyes were like a flame of fire. His feet were like burnished bronze, when it has been made to glow in a furnace, and His voice was like the sound of many waters. In His right hand He held seven stars, and out of His mouth came a sharp two-edged sword; and His face was like the sun shining in its strength.
>
> When I saw Him, I fell at His feet like a dead man. And He placed His right hand on me, saying, "Do not be afraid; I am the first and the last, and the living One; and I was dead, and behold, I am alive forevermore, and I have the keys of death and of Hades." Revelation 1:12–18

John fell on his face, overwhelmed by an encounter with the glorified Son of God. And if John—a close friend of Jesus who had been cleansed by the power of His blood—could not stand in His presence, how can we dare to treat the Lord casually?

WISDOM

Why do I present such challenging thoughts near the beginning of this book? Simply put, I have learned that the timeless message of Proverbs 9:10 rings ever true:

> The fear of the Lord is the beginning of wisdom,
> And the knowledge of the Holy One is understanding.
> Proverbs 9:10

We are vulnerable souls, and in the depths of our hearts we want to know and experience our Creator's amazing love. However, it is not the love of God, but the fear of the Lord, that is the beginning of wisdom. Any view of love or grace that minimizes heavenly authority or denies the consequences of sin will distort our vision.

People do not think the way God thinks. When we present a one-dimensional view of His love, selfish hearts easily confuse love with license. Consider our human construct of Santa Claus, for example. Santa wants us to be good, but only blinks an eye at our transgressions. In the end, he blesses regardless of our actions. I think Santa Claus is pretty close to what most Americans want God to be.

The Almighty never conforms to our expectations, and His wisdom is not something we could ever control. *The instant the human will begins to exert its influence, wisdom ceases to be divine.*

What prevents us from confusing God's unconditional love with a license to do as we please? A healthy fear of the Lord. He is all-powerful and sovereign—the highest authority possible. And He reigns as the righteous and just Judge who will one day hold all humanity accountable without bias or partiality.

If we want to truly know God, to walk in His ways and grow in His grace, a deep and sincere reverence for our Creator is the place to begin.

THE BOTTOM LINE

Knowing our Savior's love is essential for life. And while we always want to rest secure in His abundant grace, the path to spiritual maturity involves an arduous journey requiring a healthy respect for the powers involved. We should consider any theological perspective that abandons a reverential fear of God to be a near miss at best. After all, we are dealing with the Creator of our cosmos—not playing horseshoes.

RELEVANT QUESTIONS

1. What is a "theological near miss"?
2. What are the dangers of a theological near miss regarding the gospel?
3. How can culture influence our perspective of Biblical truth?
4. Please read Exodus 19:16–19. How would you have reacted had you been present?
5. Have you ever had a terrifying experience with nature?
6. What is the difference between being terrified of God and having a healthy fear of God?
7. Please read Isaiah 6:1–7 and give your perspective.
8. What do you think about Revelation 19:11–16?
9. What is the difference in John's perspective between John 13:21–25 and Revelation 1:12–18?
10. Why would the Bible teach that the fear of the Lord, rather than the love of the Lord, is the beginning of wisdom?

CHAPTER FIVE

PRESENTING RELEVANT MESSAGES

When you read "Presenting Relevant Messages," what comes to mind? Perhaps you think I am encouraging pastors to wear ripped jeans that look like they got attacked by a wild animal. Or maybe to preach with fog rising from the stage. Or perhaps you believe I am speaking of current events and incorporating the weekly news cycle into sermons. Actually, I had none of these in mind. The Bible possesses a relevance that transcends time. Allow me to illustrate.

My first car was a maroon 1975 Chevy Vega with an aluminum block engine and three-speed standard transmission—not exactly a mark of coolness in that era. To make matters worse, the vehicle had spent about a year and a half sitting without use. That season of neglect caused the clutch cable to become rusted and pitted.

A pitted clutch cable meant that shifting gears on the three-speed transmission felt a lot like lifting weights. With seemingly all my leg strength (which was not much to begin with), I would push the clutch pedal to the floor and make the shift. Then I would attempt to gently release the pedal until hitting the *friction point*, at which time the transmission would engage. But smooth and gentle shifts took place mostly in my imagination. Because the clutch was so stiff, I usually jerked and jolted my way through our small town. What a legendary vehicle that was!

SPIRITUAL FRICTION POINTS

As standard transmissions become less common, the concept of a friction point loses its meaning. Still, it provides an excellent illustration regarding the relevance of God's Word.

The friction point is where something begins to happen. With the clutch to the floor, a driver can press the gas pedal as hard as he or she wants, and the revving engine will take the car nowhere. But once the clutch hits its friction point, the transmission engages and movement immediately results.

We all have "friction points" in our lives. I am referring to places with the potential to bring real change as we journey through life on this earth. And if we want to help people grow toward spiritual maturity, we must effectively engage their friction points with God's Word.

Pastors generally preach the Word to move people toward desired behavior. In contrast, teachers often convey important information intending to educate. But for preaching and teaching to be truly effective, they must also unlock an understanding of Biblical concepts that are relevant to daily living.

As important as salvation is, a pastor who preaches only about the need to be saved and go to heaven will soon lose the attention of a congregation. And if people do not engage with the Scriptures, they will wallow in immaturity. All kinds of problems then result, and the idea of spiritual maturity becomes little more than a delusion.

The Bible is both timeless and relevant to daily life because its pages address the issues that affect us most. We just need to look for those connections. And when we address relevant issues wisely, our people will have an opportunity to engage with truth and move forward in their growth.

Think for a minute about the issues you and your family struggle with most. Specifically, I am referring to the struggles of daily life apart from church leadership. Perhaps it involves the challenges of making financial ends meet, finding rest, or building meaningful relationships. Or maybe we are talking about a struggle with worry, a temptation to control, or a nagging desire for significance. These are all friction-point issues that profoundly influence our spiritual growth.

A HUMBLE POSTURE

Humble authenticity is a primary key to touching spiritual friction points effectively. We do our people no favors when we fall prey to the temptation to portray ourselves as perfect leaders. Not only does such an approach put us out of touch with the everyday person, but it also places us on a pedestal. Seeing our image of perfection and the high vantage point from which we communicate, our listeners begin to believe they can never attain to our lofty standards. Being viewed with a sense of awe might stroke our egos, but this type of thinking also hinders their growth, leading to both apathy and spiritual immaturity. If we want to move people forward in their faith, we cannot do it while standing high and aloof.

A friend of mine recently sent out a group email inquiring about recommendations for a plumber. He had a minor issue to resolve and was looking to hire someone for the project. "Russ," I responded, "no need to hire someone. We can figure that out." When I next saw Russ, a wry smile revealed his excitement. "When I saw your message, I thought that if that moron Bob can do it, I can too!" Those might not have been Russ's exact words, but I think you get the idea. A few days later, my friend completed the project in less than ten minutes—and with no assistance.

At about that time, I heard a speaker who was a gifted and polished communicator. And he was not shy in broadcasting his abilities. Just about all of us came away in awe, thinking we could never attain to his level.

If your leadership were to be characterized by one of these scenarios, which would it be? Is your goal to *inspire* or *impress*? When people look at your life, do they come away inspired to serve? Does your humble example encourage them to take uncomfortable steps forward? Or does your unattainable standard leave them in awe and inactive?

Our listeners need to see our humanity, which includes our shortcomings and struggles. At the same time, we want to be careful to avoid anything too raw. Not everyone can handle the reality of your present imperfections. As has often been said, "It's better to show them your scars than your wounds."

Isolation can be deadly, and even pastors need trusted friends to help navigate seasons of adversity. But raw wounds are best revealed to close friends and counselors. Because so much is at stake, those intimate struggles require wisdom, trust, and faithful support. Most deep, personal, raw issues are not suitable for public display because people will respond in all kinds of unhealthy ways. We can, however, share publicly about the struggles that we have already navigated, the lessons we have learned, and the relevant hope we have discovered in the process.

I do not see this approach as fake or insincere. Leaders are just as human as everyone else, which means we are also vulnerable. How we need wisdom to protect ourselves from being overwhelmed by the dynamics of spiritual leadership!

CUT FROM THE SAME CLOTH

Some of our struggles are unique to spiritual leadership, but we also have much in common with all humanity. *Leading is not as much about standing on a platform as it is successfully navigating trials and tribulations before everyone else.* When we press into God through our struggles, we find divine wisdom to help others grow in His grace. It is here that the heart of relevant preaching and teaching lies.

I am not suggesting that anyone abandon expository preaching or focus entirely on personal experience. But I am saying that the Word of God must become *incarnate* in our own lives. As the Word of God manifests in us, our messages will

PRESENTING RELEVANT MESSAGES

become more relevant and they will more effectively connect with our listeners.

THE BOTTOM LINE

Spiritual growth requires relevant messages that hit the friction points in people's lives. Not only must we preach and teach the Word, we must do so in relevant ways that come alongside our listeners. Transformation comes not simply from hearing the Word preached, but by engaging with God through issues that are relevant to daily living.

RELEVANT QUESTIONS

1. What is your experience with driving a standard transmission vehicle?
2. What do you think about the friction point concept in regard to relevance?
3. What friction points can you identify in people's lives?
4. Why is it important to help people unlock an understanding of God's ways?
5. What role does humility play in the effectiveness of our preaching and teaching?
6. Does your style of leadership cause people to be inspired or impressed?
7. What do you think of, "It's better to show them your scars than your wounds"?
8. Can you think of a past personal struggle that has brought life and encouragement to others?
9. Do you have someone to help you process your raw issues? If not, what steps can you take in that direction?
10. What does it mean for the Word of God to become incarnate in our lives?

CHAPTER SIX

STARTING AT THE BEGINNING

A wise pastor once told me that everyone's logic makes sense if you understand the person's starting point. That statement stuck with me and seems more accurate as time passes.

A relevant example would be abortion. For most devoted Christians, the starting point is Genesis 1:1: "In the beginning, God created the heavens and the earth." Not only are we accountable to a higher authority, we also value the life God created in His image (Genesis 1:27). And knowing His goodness and power, we believe He can redeem even the worst circumstances.

What is the starting point for an unbeliever? It often stems from a naturalistic, evolutionary paradigm taught in schools. If naturalism is true, we are insignificant, alone, and without meaning in this vast cosmos. All we have is our short time on a "survival of the fittest" planet. Should it surprise us when society finds its highest value in *Me*? Anything threatening *my* happiness or well-being is perceived as a threat. The more noble-minded might contend for the well-being of our planet, but they still think as if adrift in a cosmic sea without a God to help or save us.

GENESIS

If we want to help people grow to spiritual maturity, we must help them understand God's ways, and to understand God's ways, we begin with the Bible's starting point: *The Book of Genesis*.

When I teach about key Christian concepts, I often begin with early Genesis. In chapters 1 and 2, we see the story of creation and a view of God apart from the sin-stained distortions that cloud modern vision. In chapters 3 and 4, we uncover the origins of sin and keys to unlock the mysteries of human behavior. Throughout the rest of Genesis, we establish the groundwork for God's redemptive story.

The creation story in Genesis contains hints of science, but it was not written as a scientific document. When we use Genesis to argue about scientific issues, such as old earth versus young earth hypotheses, we create unnecessary distractions that hinder us from addressing what matters most.

Imagine covering the sidewalk to a church door with large rocks that people must crawl over just to get to the door. How many might walk away without ever hearing the message of eternal life? Is it not best to remove as many obstacles as possible so people can come face to face with the truth?

Why were the Scriptures penned? Not to address scientific issues, but to bring people closer to God, grow them to maturity, and equip them for service.

> All Scripture is inspired by God and profitable for teaching, for reproof, for correction, for training in righteousness; so that the man of God may be adequate, equipped for every good work. 2 Timothy 3:16–17

The entire Bible, Genesis included, centers on the relationship between God and humanity. Furthermore, most scientific studies about origins are highly speculative because it is impossible to establish proof through experimentation. This is especially true regarding our cosmos. I think Christians should be curious and welcome scientific study, but we must hold opinions about origins loosely. And from a textual perspective, the integrity of the Bible does not depend upon young earth theories.

Having been a chemist before going into ministry, I value analytical thinking. But we must apply it in the proper context. I have found the relational dynamics of early Genesis to contain far more relevant and essential knowledge than any scientific exploration of the text. But how many educated people get that far? Only as we move beyond the distractions and study Genesis for its intended purposes can we unpack the issues influencing a potential relationship with God.

GENESIS IS RELEVANT

In the modern church, the term "relevant" often means fashionable clothing, trendy backdrops, and upbeat music. I am not against any of these (although no one has ever accused me of being a fashion icon). But nothing is more relevant than the Word of God because it meets us where we live. This is especially true of early Genesis and key themes such as *identity, fruitfulness, freedom, fear, pride, redemption, shame, and stewardship.*

People in this world are diverse; I will give you that. But we are also similar. Everyone, for example, longs for a sense of identity that feels significant. By highlighting such themes from a Biblical context, we can preach the Word while connecting with people at the core of their beings. I am not just referring to emotional messages that tug on the heartstrings, although we might need those sometimes. In so many ways, the good news of the gospel is an identity message. Salvation is not just about where we go after death, but also about who we become in this life.

Key Biblical themes remain relevant to our day, and they continue to *transform* human lives. A study about identity begun in Genesis 1 and 2 will lead us to the New Testament gospel of grace and newfound freedom from human approval. But identity is far from the only relevant issue. As another meaningful example, a study on fruitfulness begun in the first chapter of Genesis will prompt us to redefine our understanding of success, which leads to a fresh path for living.

THE BOTTOM LINE

While we can enjoy expounding upon topics such as identity and fruitfulness, we also understand they are part of a bigger picture—one that begins in Genesis. Incorporating Genesis into our teaching and preaching makes the Bible relevant and helps people see the greater whole of God's plan at work in our world. If we want people to flourish in their faith, we cannot ignore what transpired at the beginning.

RELEVANT QUESTIONS

1. What do you think of the statement, "Everybody's logic makes sense if you understand the person's starting point"?
2. What role does the book of Genesis play in helping us understand God's ways?
3. Why is it a mistake to view Genesis through a modern scientific lens?
4. How can Genesis 1 and 2 help us see God more clearly?
5. How do Genesis 3 and 4 help us know humanity better?
6. What are some ways in which people are diverse?
7. What are some ways in which people are similar?
8. How do the following themes factor into early Genesis?
    a. Identity
    b. Freedom
    c. Fear
    d. Redemption
9. What other themes from early Genesis do you think are highly relevant to people today?
10. What is necessary to help people see the big picture of God's plan for humanity?

Section Two

Discerning the Way Forward

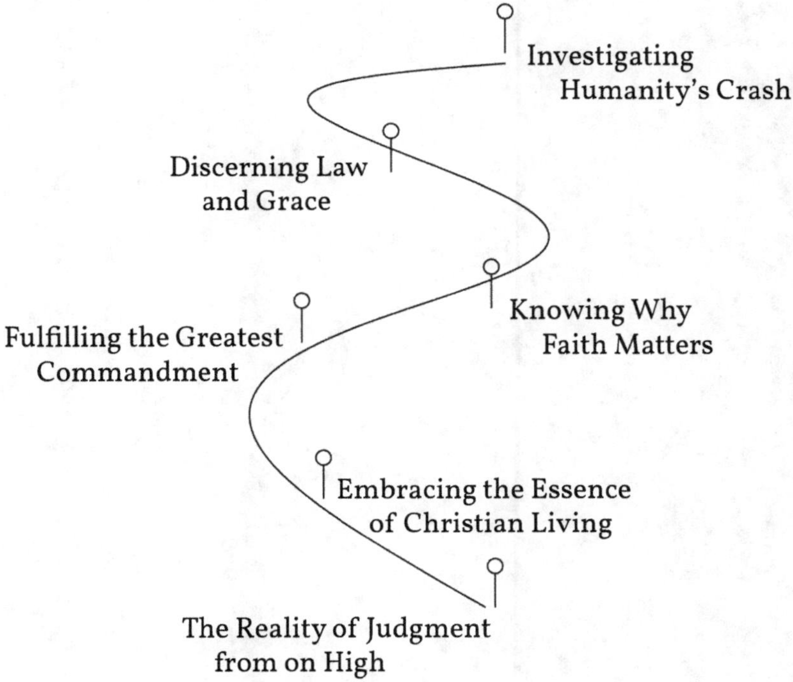

- Investigating Humanity's Crash
- Discerning Law and Grace
- Knowing Why Faith Matters
- Fulfilling the Greatest Commandment
- Embracing the Essence of Christian Living
- The Reality of Judgment from on High

All Scripture is inspired by God and profitable for teaching, for reproof, for correction, for training in righteousness; so that the man of God may be adequate, equipped for every good work.

2 Timothy 3:16–17

CHAPTER SEVEN

INVESTIGATING HUMANITY'S CRASH

The first two chapters of Genesis display a majestic view of God unstained by the sin and corruption of this world. Genesis 3 then provides profound insight into the root issues of human nature. In particular, we can learn much from the fall of humanity. I often refer to it as "the crash" because of the vast amount of collateral damage involved.

Although much remains shrouded in mystery, the Holy Spirit opens our eyes to what transpired beneath the branches of the tree of the knowledge of good and evil. Specifically, within the temptation presented by the serpent in the garden of Eden, we can identify several lies and half-truths. Out of these, the primary roots of human sin sprout. From the forbidden tree come the poisonous roots of unbelief, death, deception, idolatry, lust, and one of the most destructive of all: pride.

THE SERPENT'S HISS

The root of pride stems from what I call "the Big Lie." This outrageous claim continues to corrupt humanity at its core. What is the Big Lie? "You will be like God." No greater deception exists. And if we read between the lines just a little, we get, "You will be like God *apart from* God." The Big Lie combines a message of self-deification with one of independence from the Wellspring of Life.

Gleaning from Revelation 12:9, we learn that the devil took form in the body of a serpent. How much the serpent resembled those of today, we do not know because this is the same devil who disguises himself as an angel of light (2 Corinthians 11:14). Jesus said that his dark agenda involves stealing, killing, and destroying (John 10:10), but how did he sink to such depths? How could such a glorious angel develop such hideous desires?

The "near and far" prophecies found in Isaiah 14 and Ezekiel 28 speak volumes. Lucifer (Latin for "light bearer") was once a great and majestic angel, perhaps the most beautiful of all. Intoxicated by the glory of heaven, he hatched a plan to overthrow the King of Glory and take His throne. A foolish coup attempt against the kingdom of God failed miserably, and the Lord cast him from heaven like burned-out fireworks. Landing on the earth, the devil repurposed his own temptation into a stumbling block for humanity.

> "How you have fallen from heaven,
> O star of the morning, son of the dawn!
> You have been cut down to the earth,
> You who have weakened the nations!
> "But you said in your heart,
> 'I will ascend to heaven;
> I will raise my throne above the stars of God,
> And I will sit on the mount of assembly
> In the recesses of the north.
> 'I will ascend above the heights of the clouds;
> I will make myself like the Most High.'"
> Isaiah 14:12–14

Rephrasing this passage into a single sentence, we read, "I will ascend to the throne of heaven by my own sufficiency!" Further condensing gives us simply, "I will ascend!" This temptation, which contains the core elements of pride, embodied the serpent's hiss.

The Bible says much about sin, and some pastors routinely address the topic from the pulpit—as they should. But preachers often struggle to address the problem of pride. We can speak of sin in a broad and general sense with relative ease, but pride strikes at the root of our personhood. Devoted leaders can sometimes feel hypocritical preaching against a temptation that trips them up time and time again.

FOUR ELEMENTS OF PRIDE

If we think about who God is, Lucifer's "I will ascend by my own sufficiency!" proclamation reveals much. Even more insight flows as we realize how humanity has also owned the phrase.

- **I** – God is at the center of the universe. If I want to be God, I become self-centered and selfish.

- **Will** – God is sovereign over all. If I want to be God, I champion my will and seek to control the people and circumstances around me.

- **Ascend** – God is glorious. If I want to be God, I seek to rise above others by finding goodness within myself apart from Him. If knocking people down a few pegs helps my cause, then so be it! But if I cannot rise according to my expectations, self-loathing will be my lot.

- **By my own sufficiency** – I will do all the above through *my* ability and strength.

Talk about relevant! When we focus on the primary causes of the human condition, we see the tangled roots of pride spreading in every direction. And if ever there was a spiritual friction point affecting virtually every area of life, this is it. No one is immune to pride, and no one can claim to have achieved total mastery over its temptations.

THE KINGDOM OF GOD

Many churches have declined in the West by allowing self-centeredness to taint the purity of the gospel message. All too often, we fixate on what *we* want out of a service. We fight battles for control when the goal should be to welcome the rule and authority of God's kingdom. Even while singing His praises, we can pursue church involvement as a means of self-validation. And as we check items off a list of heaven's supposed expectations, feelings of self-righteousness rise like a church steeple into the sky. What appears to be pious religiosity can often be fueled by insidious pride.

Teaching about pride and its four subroots will get people's attention because we are all affected. Yes, Jesus died on the cross to save us from our sins, but the Christian faith is never about us. And though our Lord modeled the life of a servant, God does not hover about, waiting to serve our every desire. We might want to make church life about us, but doing so exacts a steep price from the integrity of our mission. Truly wise preaching will have none of it. Instead, perceptive leaders will strive to establish the culture of God's kingdom within our churches.

When teaching about pride, I often appeal to my listeners' love for Christ. Those who recognize its deadly influence on their hearts will yield to the Lord even when it hurts. But people who view themselves as demigods will continue to vie for control even when aware of its sinfulness. This distinction helps separate those who love the Lord from those putting on a religious show. Be forewarned, however: neither humans nor demons relinquish "their" territory without a fight. Conflict will never be far off when God's kingdom advances on earth.

We can confront pride by teaching from early Genesis, and we can also attack its roots by illuminating *the Lord's Prayer* (Matthew 6:9–13). God never intended this unique prayer for mindless repetition. Its astute wisdom confronts all four elements of human pride. We can say something similar about the Sabbath, but in a more subtle way.[1] As our eyes open to these dynamics, the wisdom of Scripture shines forth.

Finally, a careful study of the New Testament will show that Jesus and His followers did not merely preach a gospel of salvation (as in going to heaven someday); they preached *the gospel of the kingdom* (Matthew 24:14). People can make a selfish grab for salvation, but kingdom preaching creates a culture of surrender in which God's will becomes our highest goal. Yes, Jesus died for us, but genuine spirituality is never about us.

THE BOTTOM LINE

If done wisely, confronting the problem of pride will have a powerful influence, not only in bringing people to Christ, but also in helping them grow to maturity. This is how we set the stage for our churches to flourish as we help believers, young and old, align with the culture of the kingdom of heaven.

RELEVANT QUESTIONS

1. Why would Lucifer have been tempted to overthrow God and take His throne?
2. Please read Genesis 3:1-6. How are people today affected by the following lies and half-truths found in the serpent's temptation?
   a. God cannot be trusted - unbelief.
   b. You will not die - death.
   c. You will become wise - deception.
   d. God is not enough to meet your needs - idolatry.
   e. Because the tree looks good, it will be good for you - lust.
   f. You will be like God apart from God - pride.
3. What is the "Big Lie"?

---

[1]. To learn more about the fascinating connection between pride and the Sabbath, please consider reading *The Search for Rest: Fifty Days to a More Peaceful Life*.

4. Please read Isaiah 14:12–14. How can we effectively address the four primary roots of pride?
   a. Self-centeredness
   b. Self-sovereignty
   c. Self-glorification
   d. Self-sufficiency
5. What is the difference between leading and controlling?
6. Please read Matthew 6:9–15. How does the Lord's Prayer confront the four roots of pride?
7. How does the Sabbath day confront the four roots of pride?
8. How does thinking in terms of the "gospel of the kingdom" influence our perspective?
9. Why is the advance of God's kingdom usually accompanied by conflict?

CHAPTER EIGHT

DISCERNING LAW AND GRACE

From what tree did Adam and Eve eat as they disobeyed God? It was the tree of the knowledge of *good and evil*—not the tree of the knowledge of evil. That distinction is huge! It is not just the knowledge of evil that should concern us; *the knowledge of good can also be deadly.*

Adam and Eve ate from the forbidden tree with a desire to be like God apart from God. God is inherently good, and so the human psyche demands to be seen in a positive light. Every person ever born has been bound by the need to attain a sense of self-goodness by measuring up to moral and cultural standards. Even bad behavior has its standards of "good," with the worst being lauded as the best. In a broad sense, we can refer to this self-righteous quest as "living by law."

The Bible does not provide a middle road between law and grace; it proclaims *grace* as the victorious *alternative* to living by law. But because law can be confusing to comprehend, and because law-based living is so ingrained in the human heart, few people seem to grasp the full breadth of grace. Even fewer seem to understand its dynamics.

PRIDE

In a moral context, living by law involves trying to attain to the status of God by finding goodness within ourselves apart from Him. Those who think they have succeeded become self-righteous, and those who fail struggle under the weight of guilt and condemnation. But regardless of whether we fail or succeed, the mere effort offends heaven's King because the root desire is to take His throne. We call this desire "pride"—a quality celebrated by some, but considered deadly in the Scriptures.

I have known many non-Christians to be "good" people. I am referring to the type of individuals who enable society to function well—ones who volunteer their time and treat others kindly. But every good person I have ever met was also self-righteous and judgmental. It might not have been in an arrogant, demeaning way, but make no mistake; they believed in their own goodness—especially compared to the "dregs" of society who leech off taxpayers and inflict needless pain upon others.

The problem with "good" people involves their self-righteous bent stemming from a history of measuring up to moral standards. This innate tendency toward self-righteousness through law-based standards is no minor issue. Any hint of self-goodness traces its roots to the tree of the knowledge of good and evil, and those poisonous roots have infiltrated all humanity. This is the mindset the apostle Paul was confronting when he wrote about law in a negative context.

Paul's negative references did not target the Mosaic law as much as a pursuit of *righteousness by law*. In a similar vein, morality is not the problem; it is a self-righteous mindset that concerns us. And while I would like to think that churches differ, alas, the deceptive allure of pride flourishes in religious spheres—as evidenced by judgmental attitudes. If the members of a church are self-righteous and judgmental, they prove their understanding of grace to be deficient.

MAKING SENSE OF THE OLD TESTAMENT

Understanding the nature of law-based living and its resulting pride helps us better grasp the purpose of the Old Testament, including many of God's seemingly unjust actions. Even after centuries of Christian study and education, a lack of understanding in this regard continues to abound.

In the first two chapters of Genesis, we find no judgment, only a warning to avoid eating from the tree of the knowledge of good and evil (Genesis 2:17). But eat from the tree they did, subjecting all humanity to law-based standards of good and evil. And law breeds not only pride, but also judgment for those who do not meet its exacting standards of perfection.

Why do we so often think we are good enough to appease God and gain entry into heaven's gates? Such confidence reflects profound ignorance. Apart from Jesus, no person can attain to heaven's perfection. And so, the Lord introduced the Mosaic law to reveal our need.

Through the exacting standards of old covenant law, we realize just how short we fall. And through the stories of the Old Testament, we recognize the severe nature of judgment that living by law brings. And though it might look as though the God of the Old Testament somehow differs from the God of the New Testament, no difference exists.

Judgment is humanity's default standing; anything less is because of God's mercy and grace. While entirely just, the harsh judgments of the Old Testament are meant to repulse us. They compel us to lift our vision and look to God's grace. Thus, even with the heavy-handed judgments related to the old covenant of law, the mercy of God was at work to steer us toward grace.

UNMERITED FAVOR

Some have wisely stated that mercy spares us from what we deserve, while grace gives us what we do not deserve. Through the cross of Jesus, God imparts divine favor we could never earn. Some struggle to grasp the concept, and others take offense to the message of their insufficiency, but grace is the distinctly Christian virtue that gives us any hope at all.

Grace that comes through faith in the sacrificial work of Jesus provides the only effective antidote to the toxicity of pride. Such is the beauty and power of the gospel as it opens a door to our Creator through a righteousness not our own. If we are to find any reason to boast, it is in Christ and not ourselves.

While we can identify no single key to vibrant Christian living, growing to maturity is impossible apart from grace. If we do not get this issue right, our spiritual lives will one day crash.

Furthermore, it is grace that creates a wide gulf between the Christian faith and every other belief system. Grace alone vanquishes the deadly power of pride to set the stage for a future Paradise.

GRACE IS MULTIFACETED

As great as God's unmerited favor might be, His grace embodies far more than we often realize. The apostle Peter exhorted his readers to be good stewards of the "manifold" grace of God (1 Peter 4:10). Grace is *multifaceted* and comes to us in varied forms. Too often, however, we overlook the empowering potential of grace. *Through grace, the Lord gives us the ability to both live in victory over sin and serve Him effectively.*

If we do not teach about the empowering aspects of grace, several bad things happen:

- People begin to imagine that grace is a license to do whatever they want.
- People begin to think that victorious Christian living is beyond their reach.
- People begin to believe that effective service is only for the "spiritually elite."
- Christian leadership becomes populated by the best educated and most naturally gifted.

When we limit our understanding of grace to simply God's unmerited favor, we also limit its transformational power. Yes, grace is favor, but it is also so much more. Without this realization, people begin to wrongly imagine that their lifestyle is immaterial. And not only will they lose sight of the importance of good works, they might also start to feel comfortable with sinful lifestyles.

As professing Christians remain mired in sinful living, conscientious leaders feel compelled to preach messages of *behavior modification*—or to impose rules—attempting to remedy these problems. In the end, they can preach grace but practice law in a futile effort to get people to live out their Christian faith.

A fuller perspective of grace inherently challenges our lifestyles because the idea of empowerment implies people taking action. If we want mature Christians in our midst, the multifaceted nature of grace must stand at the core of our theology—and our preaching.

THE BOTTOM LINE

I could write an entire book about law and grace (and have done so).[1] After all, the topic represents a primary focus of the apostle Paul's theology as embodied in the classic New Testament books of Romans and Galatians. Grace and transformation ever go hand in hand. And so it is that understanding the multifaceted nature of grace provides an excellent springboard from which we can launch the bulk of our Christian teaching.

RELEVANT QUESTIONS

1. Why does it matter that Adam and Eve ate from the tree of the knowledge of good and evil, and not just the tree of the knowledge of evil?

---

1. My book *The Divine Progression of Grace: Blazing a Trail to Fruitful Living* expounds upon the themes of law and grace in far greater detail.

2. How is living by law (for the sake of righteousness) related to the tree of the knowledge of good and evil?
3. How does pride relate to living by law in our human efforts to pursue righteousness?
4. How does the Mosaic law of the old covenant point us toward the new covenant gospel of grace?
5. What is the problem with being a "good" person apart from faith in Christ for salvation?
6. Why is salvation by grace through faith the only effective antidote to pride?
7. How does God's grace set Christianity apart from all other belief systems?
8. What problems are associated with a one-dimensional view of grace?
9. In what ways do pastors often preach grace but practice law?
10. In what ways does grace empower us?

CHAPTER NINE

KNOWING WHY FAITH MATTERS

When my son played Little League Baseball, a particular scenario unfolded often. Frustrated by a young pitcher throwing the ball high, a coach would yell from the dugout, "Get the ball down!" Invariably, the next pitch would bounce in the dirt. Instead of focusing on the target, the little guys routinely overreacted to previous excesses.

In chapter 5, I presented the concept of spiritual friction points that meet us where we live. Faith is one such point, and it is often rife with confusion because of past excesses and overreactive responses to those errors.

Specifically, I am referring to the excesses we have seen associated with some parts of the Word-Faith camp. In the name of faith, some people have justified all kinds of selfish and judgmental attitudes. We can find just cause to criticize such abuse of the Scriptures, but I have also seen overreactions that give ground to unbelief. Our goal should be to "live on target" by understanding and aligning with God's ways, not simply reacting to what others are saying and doing.

A PRIMARY FRICTION POINT

From start to finish, the Bible emphasizes faith in God. Habakkuk 2:4 teaches that "the righteous shall live by faith." This timeless truth resounds throughout the Old and New Testaments.

However, people naturally walk by sight rather than faith. Even worse, many Western Christians disdain the idea of living by faith. We prefer a comfortable lifestyle built upon the apparent security of a material world. To the Western mind, faith is a nice, abstract concept—until the winds of adversity begin to blow.

I have found very few Westerners who trust God as much as they think they do. Weak faith can be difficult to identify during prosperous times. But when hardship comes knocking, reactions such as anxiety, fear, and complaining will reveal shaky foundations. Unnecessary drama often follows. Consider how the people of ancient Israel responded as they traversed a desolate wilderness. Are we all that different?

> The sons of Israel said to them [Moses and Aaron], "Would that we had died by the Lord's hand in the land of Egypt, when we sat by the pots of meat, when we ate bread to the full; for you have brought us out into this wilderness to kill this whole assembly with hunger."
> Exodus 16:3

We also recognize the need to live by faith when seemingly trustworthy institutions begin to erode. Many Americans lament the loss of peace and security they experienced during times past. Their national, economic, educational, church, and family lives felt so much more stable. Even people without faith could enjoy a general sense of peace through their confidence in these institutions. Today's souls can find few human institutions on which to rest their trust. I find it no surprise that anxiety and mental health issues continue to rise to sky-high levels. The world feels out of control, with no source of security to grasp.

Those who enjoyed stability in times past might be inclined to look with contempt upon today's youth who struggle to adjust, but their histories differ vastly. Instead, we must learn to meet people in their struggles and guide them to a God who is worthy of our complete trust.

THE IMPORTANCE OF FAITH

A vital starting point for life and growth involves understanding why faith matters so much. If people do not grasp the value of faith, our Lord will appear as unjust, and perhaps cruel. Even those with a general belief in God will struggle to trust when He seems not to care.

Understanding the importance of faith begins with recognizing both divine and human desires. On God's part, relationships present the highest ideal, and we can never experience genuine intimacy apart from trust. *The gospel of Jesus Christ is not so much about a future heavenly bliss as about enjoying an intimate relationship with our Creator.* Heaven provides both the extension and fulfillment of what begins on earth.

Our natural human bent toward self-exaltation also looms large. Salvation by grace through faith in Jesus provides the only effective antidote to disarm the power of pride. This is because the work of righteousness lies outside ourselves. Through faith, the cross of Christ disarms our ability to boast.

We cannot overstate the importance of these two issues—intimacy with our Creator and disarming the power of sinful pride. We are not just talking about noble ideals, but about the difference between light and darkness, between life and death.

As with the importance of law and grace, faith is not the only thing that matters, but it is foundational in every way. All else, including our love, flows out of a wellspring of faith. If we neglect to strengthen faith today, we will pay a steep price tomorrow.

BRINGING PEOPLE ON BOARD

If trusting God is so vital to our well-being, we can understand why the Lord would go to great lengths to test and prove our faith. Is this not what we see in the lives of spiritual icons such as Abraham, David, and Paul?

Living by faith is not just for spiritual giants, though. In his first letter, the apostle Peter made clear the relationship between trials and faith:

> In this you greatly rejoice, even though now for a little while, if necessary, you have been distressed by various trials, so that the proof of your faith, being more precious than gold which is perishable, even though tested by fire, may be found to result in praise and glory and honor at the revelation of Jesus Christ. 1 Peter 1:6–7

From God's perspective, the proving of our faith means everything. Rare is the human, however, who lives with the realization that triumphant faith carries far more value than material wealth.

One of the great travesties of life occurs when people view God's faith-perfecting efforts as a sign of abandonment. Instead of getting on board with the growth process, they sink into bitter despair because He has apparently forgotten them. For those who teach and preach, a vital part of ministry stewardship involves shining a Scriptural light on this erroneous perspective.

This line of thinking brings us to another essential truth that preachers and teachers dare not miss: if we are teaching and exhorting others to trust the Lord, we must lead the way in our own day-to-day living. A necessary element of leadership involves going first and then using what we have learned to help bring others along. Having been through the fire ourselves, we are better equipped to lift people up, rather than placing them under a condescending burden of judgment and condemnation. Faith matters for everyone—in all places and at all times.

THE BOTTOM LINE

From the pulpit to the pew to our daily lives, faith influences virtually every aspect of our existence. Faith matters; there is no way around it. And as much as we might seek alternative ways, the only viable path toward growth involves cultivating a vital trust in our Lord and Savior. Such unwavering confidence in God will lead people to respond to adversity in mature ways, releasing the blessings of God while minimizing the distractions and difficulties brought about by unnecessary drama.

RELEVANT QUESTIONS

1. What makes faith a friction point for Christian growth?
2. What does Habakkuk 2:4 speak to you?
3. Why do we naturally walk by sight rather than faith?
4. What are the ramifications of walking by sight rather than faith?
5. Why do many Western Christians disdain the idea of living by faith?
6. How has the erosion of "institutional trust" affected society?
7. In what ways can fear and anxiety provide a connecting point for the gospel?
8. Why is intimacy impossible without trust?
9. How does faith provide a necessary antidote to pride?
10. How is our perception of God affected when we do not realize the value of faith?
11. What are some dangers of failing to understand that the Lord seeks to stimulate our growth through trials?
12. Why is it vital for Christian leaders and teachers themselves to be growing in faith?

CHAPTER TEN

FULFILLING THE GREATEST COMMANDMENT

The virtue of love has been preached about a million times over, yet it still warrants our attention. Sadly, the church has fallen far short of heavenly ideals throughout the centuries. One need only consider the splintered nature of our Christian expression to know the authentic love of God has not fully taken root.

Love is the greatest of all virtues. The Bible and culture converge here. The definition of love, however, can differ vastly between the church and the world. We will begin exploring that difference by considering the centrality of love in the Scriptures:

> But when the Pharisees heard that Jesus had silenced the Sadducees, they gathered themselves together. One of them, a lawyer, asked Him a question, testing Him, "Teacher, which is the great commandment in the Law?" And He said to him, "'You shall love the Lord your God with all your heart, and with all your soul, and with all your mind.' This is the great and foremost commandment. The second is like it, 'You shall love your neighbor as yourself.' On these two commandments depend the whole Law and the Prophets." Matthew 22:34–40

The greatest commandment is to love the Lord with all one's heart, soul, and mind. It is upon this commandment that everything else hinges. Loving God first makes unpolluted love possible. God is love. God defines love. And, by His grace, God empowers us to love.

LOVE MYSELF FIRST?

According to Jesus, the second greatest commandment is to "love your neighbor as yourself." It is here that our human understanding of love can depart from God's. Well-meaning Christians often say the command to love our neighbors as ourselves affirms the need to love ourselves first. After all, if we do not love ourselves, how can we love others?

When God commanded us to love our neighbors as ourselves, He assumed we *already* love ourselves, meaning we naturally prioritize our desires above others'. As an example of self-love in action, virtually all people who own a refrigerator have hidden a tasty delight in the back so no one else could eat it first.

A "love myself first" mentality corrupts the purity of love and mires us in confusion. Even the most astute Bible scholar would struggle to find a passage in Scripture that speaks about self-love in a positive light. Consider the apostle Paul's second letter to his disciple Timothy:

> But realize this, that in the last days difficult times will come. For men will be lovers of self, lovers of money, boastful, arrogant, revilers, disobedient to parents, ungrateful, unholy, unloving, irreconcilable, malicious gossips, without self-control, brutal, haters of good, treacherous, reckless, conceited, lovers of pleasure rather than lovers of God, holding to a form of godliness, although they have denied its power; Avoid such men as these. 2 Timothy 3:1–5

Paul mentions self-love first, and in the same context as descriptions such as "malicious gossips," "brutal," and "haters of good." His use of the term in this passage implies that loving ourselves first is the *source* of our woes—not the solution to them.

WHAT ABOUT SELF-HATRED?

The perspective I am presenting brings a significant (and reasonable) concern to light. Self-hatred is a problematic issue that stems from looking at oneself with disdain. So, if the answer to this destructive tendency is not self-love, what is?

We begin by realizing that what we call "self-hatred" is actually a distorted form of self-love that rejects God's goodness in a person's life. People often despise themselves because they want better for themselves. If I "hate" myself because of a wart on the bridge of my nose, for example, I am saying, "I deserve better than this!" That, my friends, is self-love. And because human nature is deceptive beyond measure, we soon despise looking at ourselves in a mirror because we do not meet desired standards.

Having wrestled with feelings of "self-hatred," I understand their destructive influence. When we disdain the undesirable, unchangeable facets of our lives, we accuse God of being uncaring: "Lord, if You really loved me, You would not have . . ." All too often, we blame God for humanity's misguided standards (Isaiah 55:6–9; 1 Samuel 16:1–7). But if we truly knew His goodness, His deep love for us, and His ability to work all things together for our good, we would recognize the Lord's desire to use even unchangeable shortcomings for our ultimate benefit.

Our Creator's love is not shallow, limited, or imperfect. Nor is it partial. I once thought that God loved others more than me, and my bitterness blinded me further to the mysterious depths of His goodness. Thankfully, His love won the day.

A BETTER WAY

What we need, rather than self-love, is to *accept ourselves* as the handiwork of a good God, beloved by our heavenly Father. How we view people, including ourselves, is generally determined by how we view our Creator. And though it can seem nearly impossible to see His love through our emotional pain, the Lord promises to turn even the worst circumstances to benefit those who truly love Him:

> And we know that God causes all things to work together for good to those who love God, to those who are called according to His purpose. Romans 8:28

What magnificent irony radiates from this brief passage! Why do we so often put ourselves first in life? We believe that self-love benefits us. But this short verse proclaims a different message. *Loving the Lord with all our heart, soul, and mind will always serve our best interests in the long run.* How typical of the God who can bring life out of death!

For those with lingering questions about this perspective of self-love, I remind you of another powerful statement Jesus made a few hours before surrendering His life to the cross:

> "A new commandment I give to you, that you love one another, even as I have loved you, that you also love one another. By this all men will know that you are My disciples, if you have love for one another." John 13:34–35

What is the difference between loving our neighbors *as ourselves* and loving one another *as Christ has loved us*? Humanity's concept of love can be twisted and tainted by self, which is why Jesus presented us with a new, *selfless* standard of love. Jesus' consistent message of self-denial, bolstered by His selfless lifestyle, leaves little doubt about His intent.

The Greek language—in which our earliest copies of the New Testament were penned—employs several words for love. The one that speaks of God's love is *agape*, which refers to an unconditional, sacrificial love that finds great value in the person being loved. This selfless standard established by Jesus leads us on a path far superior to that of self-love.

OUR BIGGER STRUGGLE

No murky waters cloud the New Testament message; Jesus-style love is selfless through and through. Our primary challenge as Christians does not involve discerning the meaning of love as much as faithfully living out a love so pure.

Loving sacrificially can seem overwhelming—especially in a world as connected as ours. Because of advances in technology, my "neighbor" might be an orphan in Africa whom I know only through a social media post. And to further complicate matters, the person presenting the plight of the orphan might actually be a scammer seeking to profit from a believer's compassion.

When presented with a myriad of issues and such overwhelming need in our world, we can easily "freeze." Unsure of what step to take next, we do nothing. Then, through repeated failures to act, we can accumulate a mountain of guilt for failing to love as we believe the Lord commands. Or we might try to hold guilt at bay by hardening our hearts.

What is the answer to this challenge? *Always love God first.* We do not need to meet every need we see; we just need to do our part in obedience to Him. And so, we cultivate faith and pray to the Lord for wisdom. By cultivating faith, we learn to trust Him to provide for our needs. And by praying for wisdom, we can get a better sense of what God wants us to do. This will protect us from being manipulated while also eliminating a foothold for guilt.

Regardless of how the Lord leads us to give and serve, we can display God's love by treating others—even our enemies—with love and respect. How our broken and divided world needs people who champion God's love even amid hatred!

When we love, we honor the Creator of all things. And when we honor Him, we set eternal blessings in motion. In the short term, it might feel as though we lose out, but God's eternal design speaks differently. No matter what we hear, see, or feel, love will eventually conquer all.

THE BOTTOM LINE

Everything begins and ends with God. And all of life revolves around loving Him first. He is both our source and model for love. We love because He first loved us. If we know His unconditional love and seek to love Him in return, He will order our steps and lead us into victory over darkness.

RELEVANT QUESTIONS

1. What are some ways in which the world's definition of love differs from God's definition?
2. Why is loving God with all one's heart, soul, and mind the first and greatest of all commandments?
3. What does it mean to love ourselves?
4. What is the problem with loving ourselves?
5. What makes "self-hatred" a distorted form of self-love?
6. What is the difference between self-love and self-acceptance?
7. How is self-hatred a rejection of God's goodness in our lives?
8. What is the significance of John 13:34?
9. What makes *agape* the highest standard of love?
10. How can living by compassion without wisdom, or following the demands of conscience open us up to manipulation?
11. Why might we freeze in the face of overwhelming need?
12. Why is cultivating faith essential to us loving others?
13. How does praying for wisdom enable us to better love God and others?
14. How can Christians walk in love even amid hatred?

CHAPTER ELEVEN

EMBRACING THE ESSENCE OF CHRISTIAN LIVING

The more I understand about the Christian faith, the more I am enamored with the wisdom of our Creator. The design of the gospel addresses the primary causes of our human condition, and it does so with *simplicity*.

In a previous chapter, we highlighted the need for people to live by grace in contrast to being bound under the dominion of law. According to the insightful apostle Paul:

> Therefore do not let sin reign in your mortal body so that you obey its lusts, and do not go on presenting the members of your body to sin as instruments of unrighteousness; but present yourselves to God as those alive from the dead, and your members as instruments of righteousness to God. For sin shall not be master over you, for you are not under law but under grace. Romans 6:12–14

Scripture emphasizes the importance of faith and love, and now that we have explored both, I want to consider how they work together to empower us to reign over sin.

> It was for freedom that Christ set us free; therefore keep standing firm and do not be subject again to a yoke of slavery.

> Behold I, Paul, say to you that if you receive circumcision, Christ will be of no benefit to you. And I testify again to every man who receives circumcision, that he is under obligation to keep the whole Law. You have been severed from Christ, you who are seeking to be justified by law; you have fallen from grace. For we through the Spirit, by faith, are waiting for the hope of righteousness. For in Christ Jesus neither circumcision nor uncircumcision means anything, but faith working through love. Galatians 5:1–6

This passage both fascinates and challenges me. But verse six shines for its simplicity. In it, we find what I identify as "the essence of Christian living": *faith working through love*, or *faith expressing itself through love*.

All of life comes down to trusting God and allowing that living faith to manifest as love. A Christian lifestyle is not about following lists of rules, but about trusting and loving.

We also need to seek heavenly wisdom because we do not always know what faith and love should look like in a particular situation. What the world calls "love" might be nothing more than hormone-induced lust. While humanity prefers to promote its own definitions of faith and love, we can reign over the power of sin only as we lean into our Creator's design.

THE TWO CROSSES

We can reframe the essence of *faith expressing itself through love* to identify closely with our Christian experience. Each of us must reckon with *two* crosses in this life. The first is the *cross of Christ* through which we receive forgiveness and through which God disarms the *power of sin*. The second is our *personal cross* of self-denial through which we put the *desires of sin* to death.

Christ's work on the cross provides the foundation upon which our relationship with God rests. Not only are we given favor in the eyes of heaven, and not only do we receive abundant grace to live in victory over sin, but faith in Christ's cross also disarms sin's power. *It is the quest for self-glorification that drives sin, so when we abandon that vain pursuit, sin loses its ability to dominate.*

The message of Christ's cross is wonderful news for the human soul, but we must still contend with sinful desires (lusts). Rarely do they pass quickly or quietly. Fleshly appetites enchant and scream and cry in a nonstop effort to compel us to yield. Therefore, we must also crucify the desires of sin by taking up a personal cross of self-denial.

> And He was saying to them all, "If anyone wishes to come after Me, he must deny himself, and take up his cross daily and follow Me. For whoever wishes to save his life will lose it, but whoever loses his life for My sake, he is the one who will save it." Luke 9:23–24

While we apply faith through the cross of Christ, we express love for God through a cross of self-denial. Love is not a feeling but a *choice* to put first those we care about. Love honors others above self, and those who love God will deny their desires to honor His. Jesus chose the imagery of the cross for a reason. Authentic love can hurt!

Death, in some form, is unavoidable—even for the Christian. Returning to the garden of Eden, we remember God's warning to Adam and Eve: "For in the day that you eat from it [the tree of the knowledge of good and evil] you will surely die" (Genesis 2:17). Thankfully, we can be spared an eternal death because of Christ's cross, but even with all Jesus has done, we cannot escape death entirely. A personal cross of self-denial remains as a necessary consequence of human sinfulness. But while a personal cross appears (and feels) sacrificial, we always benefit in the end.

Because each person is unique, so is each personal cross. What causes one person to break out in a cold sweat might go unnoticed by another. For many people, bearing a cross of self-denial means saving money instead of spending on personal desires. But for someone prone to hoarding, spending might help crucify fleshly desires of greed and control. God knows us as individuals and will tailor our circumstances accordingly.

Does carrying a cross of self-denial sound distasteful? Absolutely! Humanity invented crucifixion, but the Son of God chose that means for His sacrificial death. It was love that sent Jesus to the cross, and it is love that calls us to deny the desires of self-will. When we sacrificially deny ourselves for the sake of others, a fragrant aroma rises to heaven.

WE NEED FAITH AND LOVE

Simplicity is not the same as simplistic. Unfortunately, many Christians apply a one-dimensional approach to Christian living. Instead of recognizing the importance of both crosses, they focus either on the cross of Christ, or on a personal cross of self-denial.

Some churches overflow with people who celebrate the cross of Christ while continuing to live selfishly—elevating their desires above those of God and others. Selfish choices then lead them back into the throes of sin's bondage. We dare never forget that Christ's cross provides grace to meet our deepest points of need—not a convenient excuse to justify selfish living. A Christian might be free from the compulsion to sin, but the door of choice will always remain open as long as we dwell in these fleshly bodies.

The early church routinely baptized new believers as part of the salvation process. Yes, those souls were saved by faith rather than works, but immediate water baptism communicated a message of death to the old self-willed mindset. Sadly, pastors and evangelists often present the gospel merely as a decision to accept Christ in order to go to heaven. But we provide no benefit to unbelievers if we do not challenge them to surrender to His lordship.

Unfortunately, selfishness is not the only significant problem we face. Truly pious people willingly embrace a cross of self-denial. In doing so, they can neglect to exercise faith in the cross of Christ. And apart from our Savior's cross, the sacrifice of self-denial soon becomes a badge of self-righteousness. Apart from faith in Christ's finished work on the cross, self-denial for religious reasons will always cause human flesh to boast in itself.

Legalism—dependence on moral law over faith—often thrives in religious circles because people mistakenly believe a sacrificial lifestyle makes them acceptable to God. Self-denial, however, can never elicit heavenly favor. Rather, self-sacrifice is our love-motivated *response* to all the Lord has done for us.

THE BOTTOM LINE

We need not complicate the Christian life. Whether a person understands all the dynamics involved with the two crosses should not be our primary concern. What matters most is that they look upon the cross of Christ with faith to receive forgiveness of their sins, and that they respond to His forgiveness by subjecting the desires of the flesh to His will.

Believing in the cross of Christ and carrying one's own personal cross are *both* necessary for those who wish to abide in grace, live in victory over sin, and bear the sweet fruit of the Holy Spirit. This is the essence of faith expressing itself through love as it plays out in our daily lives. Through faith in the cross of Christ, the power of sin is disarmed. And through our individual cross of self-denial, we crucify the desires of sin. Both elements are necessary for those who wish to break free from sin's dominion and live fully fruitful lives for the glory of God.

RELEVANT QUESTIONS

1. Please read Galatians 5:1–6. What stands out to you about this passage?

2. What do you think about the idea that faith working through love is the essence of Christian living?
3. Why is it important to help people grasp the simple essence of Christian living?
4. Why do we also need wisdom when dealing with the realms of faith and love?
5. In what way does faith find its expression in the cross of Christ?
6. How does faith in the cross of Christ disarm the power of sin?
7. How does love find its expression in a personal cross of self-denial?
8. How does carrying one's personal cross mortify the desires of sin?
9. Why is carrying a personal cross of self-denial to our benefit as we seek to honor the Lord?
10. What happens if we embrace Christ's cross through faith but neglect to carry our own personal cross of self-denial?
11. What happens when we sacrificially deny ourselves but fail to exercise faith in the cross of Christ?
12. What is the significance of water baptism?

CHAPTER TWELVE

THE REALITY OF JUDGMENT FROM ON HIGH

One fall day, I wondered how the football team from my college alma mater was doing. The IUP Crimson Hawks had been highly competitive, achieving a national ranking during multiple seasons. And considering that they overcame a tough opponent in the first game of the season, I knew the second one would be interesting.

While searching for the score, a livestream of the game popped onto my screen. With the outcome closely contested, I scooched to the edge of my chair to watch the last quarter. Behind by a single point, my team marched down the field to within the opponent's five-yard line! With just seconds remaining, the Hawks called a timeout so they could kick a field goal. But, mysteriously, and to everyone's confusion, the clock expired. No more plays. No field goal. No hard-fought victory. The Hawks lost by only a point because somebody had miscounted the number of timeouts taken. The clock can be harsh, caring nothing about our feelings or intentions.

FRIEND OR FOE?

Time is either a friend or foe, depending on our relationship with God, or the lack thereof. But not everyone sees it that way. Some people assume all souls go to heaven, or that the punishment of hell is reserved for only the *really* bad—like Adolf Hitler and his henchmen.

While it is a tragic mistake to view God as harsh and demanding, we dare not forget He will one day judge the world. When humanity's time clock expires, there will be no opportunities for "do-overs." Today is our opportunity to repent and receive forgiveness. Tomorrow might tell a different story.

> Then I saw a great white throne and Him who sat upon it, from whose presence earth and heaven fled away, and no place was found for them. And I saw the dead, the great and the small, standing before the throne, and books were opened; and another book was opened, which is the book of life; and the dead were judged from the things which were written in the books, according to their deeds. And the sea gave up the dead which were in it, and death and Hades gave up the dead which were in them; and they were judged, every one of them according to their deeds. Then death and Hades were thrown into the lake of fire. This is the second death, the lake of fire. And if anyone's name was not found written in the book of life, he was thrown into the lake of fire. Revelation 20:11–15

For many in the Western world, the idea of eternal judgment seems cruel and unloving. Indeed, there are people who reject the God of the Bible for this very reason. What this tells me, however, is that they view God not as a real entity, but as an imaginary figure to be manipulated according to personal desires. If people actually knew God to be real, they would fall on their faces in repentance rather than raise their noses in contempt.

CONSIDERATIONS

Let us gain some much-needed insight by considering a broader perspective of this important concept.

- **God has every right to judge.** The Lord spoke this world into existence. As the Creator, He owns *all* the rights. No matter what we want to believe, no higher authority exists.

- **God's judgment will be just.** When reading through the Old Testament, we might question certain divine actions that appear to be cruel or unjust. The problem is not with God, but with our limited perspectives. No matter what appearances might say, the Lord would *never* do anything unjust. In fact, it is injustice that He will judge.

- **Psalm 89:14 tells us that *righteousness* and *justice* are the *foundation* of His throne.** Think about that for a minute. What would a king allow near his throne? Only what he values. The Lord celebrates justice and condemns injustice. It is not the idea of an unjust God that should concern us, but the reality of our own unjust actions.

- **Love demands judgment.** As children mature, they naturally develop a sense of morality. The specifics might differ from culture to culture, but an innate awareness of right and wrong transcends all cultures. Even people who do not believe in God will recoil with outrage if they see a vulnerable person treated unjustly.

A nation without justice soon becomes mired in corruption, and it is usually the common people who suffer most. So if we agree in principle that judgment is necessary for the sake of justice, we must also consider what types of situations warrant judgment. I can think of several obvious ones:

- **Molestation** – Would a just person ignore the rape of a woman? How about the molestation of a child?

- **Oppression** – Should we turn a blind eye to slavery or the mistreatment of indigenous peoples?

- **Exploitation** – Would a just society be okay with child labor or sex trafficking?

- **Suppression of truth** – What do we think about a government entity that suppresses truth to hide corruption? Do we not agree that such actions should be investigated and called into account?

- **Murder** – Grieving loved ones will often call for justice after a friend or family member is murdered. Do they want justice because they have cruel hearts? No. The demand for justice flows from a heart of deep love.

- **Treason** – We see universal agreement that treason is the worst possible crime against a nation. Throughout history, traitors have been condemned to death for betraying their own countries.

- **Etc., etc., etc.** – Depending upon individual perspectives, we could list many more actions that can be considered worthy of judgment. Lying, stealing, and falsely accusing an innocent person would all qualify.

God hates injustice—and especially the mistreatment of the innocent (Matthew 18:6), the vulnerable (James 5:1–6), and those who are His covenant friends (Genesis 12:3). I wonder how many people would be guilty of just these crimes against heaven?

The truth is that we are all guilty of treason against the kingdom of God. Not only did Adam and Eve join a treasonous coup attempt against the most loving and just government ever to exist, but through our pride, we have all joined in the deadly plot. Few people want to think of themselves as co-conspirators with the devil, but that is our spiritual reality. There is no such thing as a "neutral" person regarding spiritual matters. We either choose to embrace Jesus as Lord and Savior, or we labor against Him by default (Matthew 12:30). No in-between exists.

I know the content of this chapter is difficult to process; these are weighty matters, to be sure. But we must also understand that a just God cannot allow treasonous actions to go unpunished. That is why Jesus willingly paid the extreme penalty of crucifixion for our sins. Furthermore, through the cross of Christ, the core motivations of our hearts are transformed. Apart from the cross, the toxicity of pride and sin will continue to pollute even our noble-minded endeavors.

ALL THAT IS HIDDEN WILL BE REVEALED

How many sins does it take to make one a sinner? Only one. And who among us can be deemed innocent of all sin? We might manage to hide our transgressions from other people, but nothing escapes heaven's notice.

> "But there is nothing covered up that will not be revealed, and hidden that will not be known. Accordingly, whatever you have said in the dark will be heard in the light, and what you have whispered in the inner rooms will be proclaimed upon the housetops." Luke 12:2–3

With the rise of DNA testing, we have seen more and more "cold cases" being solved by law enforcement. People who thought they got away with murder are being exposed like never before through DNA profiling. But even those who escape justice on this earth must one day give an eternal account for their actions.

WILLFUL SINNERS?

Much of the issue of judgment centers on the human will. Having created humanity in His image, the Lord has given us each the freedom and capacity to love. That also means He has given us the freedom to act selfishly. Our freedoms, however, are not absolute. Ultimately, we will each give an account to our Creator for what we did and did not do.

A simple but challenging question stands worthy of consideration: Who do I love more, God or myself?

Sometimes we sin out of ignorance. At other times, a spiritual stronghold might leave us conflicted—compelling us to sin even when we want to do otherwise (Romans 7:14–25). In these types of situations, God can be amazingly patient with our wayward souls (Romans 8:1–2).

But sinful actions can also come from stubborn, willful choices (Hebrews 3:12–15). We want what we want regardless of what God thinks. For lovers of self, specific actions are almost secondary. It is the stubborn, underlying attitude of the heart that invites judgment. So, before questioning whether specific actions are sinful, wisdom calls us to contemplate the motives behind those actions.

How much simpler life would be if only non-Christians sinned willfully! But for whatever reason, even seasoned believers can feel as though grace has given them a license to sin. And though this mindset might be fairly common, it is also dangerous. According to the writer of Hebrews:

> For if we go on sinning willfully after receiving the knowledge of the truth, there no longer remains a sacrifice for sins, but a terrifying expectation of judgment and THE FURY OF A FIRE WHICH WILL CONSUME THE ADVERSARIES. Anyone who has set aside the Law of Moses dies without mercy on the testimony of two or three witnesses. How much severer punishment do you think he will deserve who has trampled under foot the Son of God, and has regarded as unclean the blood of the covenant by which he was sanctified, and has insulted the Spirit of grace? For we know Him who said, "VENGEANCE IS MINE, I WILL REPAY." And again, "THE LORD WILL JUDGE HIS PEOPLE." It is a terrifying thing to fall into the hands of the living God. Hebrews 10:26–31

While I do not entirely understand the dynamics involved with sinning stubbornly, I fear the potential consequences. People who think they fool God fool only themselves. There is not anything beyond the knowledge or understanding of our Creator.

> For the word of God is living and active and sharper than any two-edged sword, and piercing as far as the division of soul and spirit, of both joints and marrow, and able to judge the thoughts and intentions of the heart. And there is no creature hidden from His sight, but all things are open and laid bare to the eyes of Him with whom we have to do. Hebrews 4:12–13

The God who created the heavens and the earth knows even our deepest thoughts. The images we project mean nothing. Whether hidden or displayed for all to see, stubborn sin leads to dire consequences. And so it is that we should always view God's grace as a gift but never a license to do whatever pleases our fleshly desires.

WHAT ABOUT THOSE WHO HAVE NOT HEARD?

We cannot address every imaginable scenario, but we know God acts justly in all He does. Regarding those born before the time of Christ, Peter alludes to the idea that Jesus preached the gospel in Hades during the span between His death on the cross and His resurrection from the dead (1 Peter 3:19–20).

But if a person never has an opportunity to hear the gospel of Jesus Christ, God deserves no blame. An honest survey of human history will show people erecting barrier after barrier against the Christian message. From making the Bible illegal, to forcing Christian expression out of the public arena, it is humans who have kept the good news of the gospel from other humans.

We must also understand that even though no person can be justified by his or her good works, degrees of judgment will vary.

Some Christians proclaim all sins to be equal, but that is not what the Bible teaches. Yes, all sin is worthy of death, but some sins carry a greater weight of judgment (John 19:11). This is especially true of those who know the truth and choose to reject—or even suppress—it (Matthew 11:21–22; Luke 12:46–48).

For the person who still struggles with the idea of God judging someone who has never heard the gospel, I might ask some simple questions. Why do you care? Is it possible that your heart is burdened because God is calling *you* to the mission field? Jesus gave His life for the spiritually lost. Are you willing to obey His call and do the same? If you refuse His will and they perish as a result, how can God be to blame?

JUDGMENT AS FRUIT

Eternal judgment is the *fruit* of what we sow during our time on earth. This idea might sound bad, but it need not be. Jesus paid a steep price on the cross so the account for our sinful actions might be wiped clean. Christians who have been cleansed by the eternal blood of Christ will be judged for their *good works*, but only for the purpose of *rewarding* them (Matthew 6:4; Hebrews 9:28). This type of judgment reflects our Creator's desire. He wants no one to perish but desires that all be rewarded richly (2 Peter 3:9).

Heaven's King remains sovereign over all things, but within that authority, He has also given us freedom to choose evil over good and to suffer the resulting consequences. Admittedly, I do not fully understand the dynamics of an eternal hell, but I believe it to be an amplification of a life separated from God—similar to the darkness and chaos we see on earth, but in greater measure.

Divine judgment is never indiscriminate. The kingdom of God has a unique culture that He has established for good and just reasons. We either seek to understand and embrace that culture and its standards, or we do not. Judgment, then, is primarily a matter of the Lord calling into account the choices we make during our time on this earth (Galatians 6:7–8).

THE BOTTOM LINE

I have written more than I intended about the topic of judgment, but the length is warranted because of the gravity of the issue. This is a weighty topic, and it is reasonable for people to have questions. We cannot answer them all fully in this short space, but we can embrace two connected truths. First, all our Creator does is righteous and just—no matter how it appears from our limited perspective. And second, the coming judgment will be the fruit of choices we have made on earth. Rather than take offense to what might seem like an unfair punishment, would it not be better to thoroughly consider the choices we are making today?

RELEVANT QUESTIONS

1. What right does God have to judge?
2. How do we know that God's judgment will be just?
3. Why does love demand judgment?
4. What are some situations in which judgment is warranted?
5. What did Jesus' sacrifice on the cross accomplish on our behalf?
6. Why will no one escape justice in the end?
7. What is the motivation behind willful sin?
8. Who is to blame for those who have never had an opportunity to hear the gospel?
9. What is the significance of Galatians 6:7–8?
10. Is time your friend or your foe?

Section Three

Growing in Faith

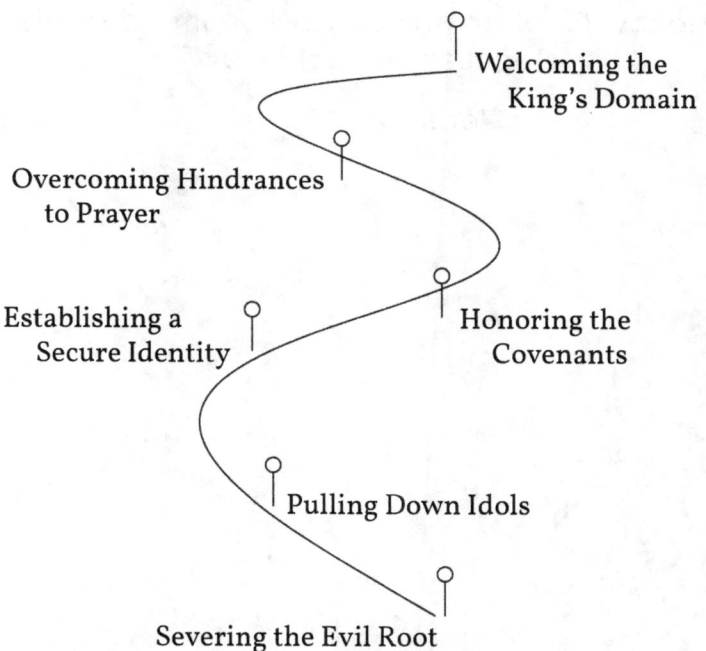

Thus says the Lord,
"Cursed is the man who trusts in mankind
And makes flesh his strength,
And whose heart turns away from the Lord.
"For he will be like a bush in the desert
And will not see when prosperity comes,
But will live in stony wastes in the wilderness,
A land of salt without inhabitant.
"Blessed is the man who trusts in the Lord
And whose trust is the Lord.
"For he will be like a tree planted by the water,
That extends its roots by a stream
And will not fear when the heat comes;
But its leaves will be green,
And it will not be anxious in a year of drought
Nor cease to yield fruit."

Jeremiah 17:5–8

CHAPTER THIRTEEN

WELCOMING THE KING'S DOMAIN

I sometimes marvel at how the US church can have so much and yet so little. In the history of this world, there has never been a nation with such a combination of wealth and Biblically-based resources within its grasp. And yet, the weakness of the church has been on full display as it has struggled to navigate spiritual decay from within and a torrent of ungodliness from without.

We can attribute a significant part of the problem to our perception of the *gospel*—the good news of Jesus Christ. Specifically, I think we have erred by removing the gospel from its New Testament context.

An array of evangelical churches present the gospel as a means of receiving forgiveness of our sins so we can one day go to heaven. A few outliers wisely focus on the importance of a personal relationship with God, rather than simply a desired future destination. However, another vital element of the gospel remains ignored or inaccurately presented: *the kingdom of God*.

THE AUTHORITY OF GOD'S KINGDOM

The recognition of a kingdom assumes the existence of a king. And in this case, we speak of a heavenly King who reigns over all. Whether people believe in Him or not, all remain subject under the realm of His authority.

The call to bend the knee before a divine King provides a very different perspective than receiving a gift of salvation as a "free ticket" to heaven. The latter allows room for a consumer mindset to flourish, while the former makes no provision of the kind. Perhaps that is why Jesus began and ended His earthly ministry by preaching and teaching about the kingdom of God:

> Now after John had been taken into custody, Jesus came into Galilee, preaching the gospel of God, and saying, "The time is fulfilled, and the kingdom of God is at hand; repent and believe in the gospel." Mark 1:14–15

> To these He also presented Himself alive after His suffering, by many convincing proofs, appearing to them over a period of forty days and speaking of the things concerning the kingdom of God. Acts 1:3

The word *gospel* means "good news," and it was the good news of the kingdom that our Lord preached. Jesus was not self-exalting, but neither did He hesitate to assert His authority as the King of the universe. Those who view the Son of God only through the lens of a meek and gracious servant to humanity do so at great peril.

When a person being ruled by the monarchy of Self comes face to face with the one true King of heaven and earth, something must change. Thus, the necessity of repentance. To ignore this dynamic for fear of offending human sensibilities is to do a grave injustice to both man and God.

THE NATURE OF THE KINGDOM

Another issue that hinders our proclamation of God's kingdom stems from a failure to understand its true nature. Throughout the centuries, well-meaning leaders have attempted to establish civil governments ruled by Biblical laws. Others have proclaimed the coming of God's kingdom as a pathway to material wealth. And still others as something that only the poor can understand or experience. All these efforts miss the mark. The Lord's heavenly kingdom is of a different nature, and operates by different principles, than any government on earth.

> Now having been questioned by the Pharisees as to when the kingdom of God was coming, He answered them and said, "The kingdom of God is not coming with signs to be observed; nor will they say, 'Look, here it is!' or, 'There it is!' For behold, the kingdom of God is in your midst." Luke 17:20–21

> Jesus answered, "My kingdom is not of this world. If My kingdom were of this world, then My servants would be fighting so that I would not be handed over to the Jews; but as it is, My kingdom is not of this realm." John 18:36

> For the kingdom of God is not eating and drinking, but righteousness and peace and joy in the Holy Spirit. Romans 14:17

The kingdom of God is spiritual in nature, and it must be advanced by spiritual—as opposed to fleshly or political—means. At the heart of that effort is *prayer*. Political efforts have their place, but focus primarily on civil laws that are imposed from without. Because participation in God's kingdom is voluntary, its advancement involves *a change of heart* from within. The great temptation for those who wade into the political arena is that its nasty underbelly hardens their hearts and deadens their love. When is the last time you heard a political candidate call for loving one's enemies?

As the apostle Paul wisely stated, we battle not against flesh and blood but against the spiritual forces of wickedness in heavenly places (Ephesians 6:10–12). Meaningful efforts to advance the kingdom will always create conflict because dark spiritual forces will fight tooth and nail to maintain their grip on power. Even so, those who walk in love are destined to triumph in victory. Every kingdom of this earth will pass, while God's benevolent rule endures forever.

> In the days of those kings the God of heaven will set up a kingdom which will never be destroyed, and that kingdom will not be left for another people; it will crush and put an end to all these kingdoms, but it will itself endure forever. Daniel 2:44

The bigger question is not whether the kingdom of God will triumph, but exactly who will become citizens of the kingdom. The quest for souls stands at the center of this great battle we fight, which is why our witness for Christ should always hold a higher place in our hearts than our political affiliation.

CREATING A KINGDOM CULTURE

As ambassadors for Christ (2 Corinthians 5:20), God has commissioned us to create a *kingdom culture* within our families and churches. In doing so, we welcome the life of God into our midst. But if that life is absent, it falls upon our shoulders to change wayward hearts, work out difficult situations, and meet overwhelming needs.

The kingdom of God is no mere add-on to the Christian faith. In the Parable of the Sower, Jesus spoke about seeds being planted in four types of soil (Matthew 13:1–23). We mostly focus on those various soil types, which is entirely appropriate. Still, there is more to the story.

Interpreting the parable for His disciples, Jesus referred to the seed as the "word—or message—of the kingdom." It should come as no surprise, then, that Jesus, His disciples, and the apostle Paul all preached about the kingdom of God. And if we want to help our people grow to spiritual maturity, it should be a primary topic for us as well.

What the world needs today is not a humanistic or even programmatic church agenda. *What the world needs is the advancement of God's kingdom through the faith-filled prayers and authentic witness of its citizens.* The rise of His kingdom breaks spiritual strongholds and puts evil in its place—under the foot of divine authority. We can experience the dynamics of the kingdom today and will enjoy it in full with the return of Christ.

THE BOTTOM LINE

The gospel we preach should proclaim a message of salvation from sin, but also the opportunity to become faithful citizens in God's everlasting kingdom. We do not want to complicate the gospel message, but if the elements of lordship and repentance are lacking, something is off.

The kingdom of God is advancing on earth and will continue to do so until the day Christ returns to establish its fullness. With the kingdom comes transformation as the life and power of heaven visit our planet. Strongholds fall, relationships are restored, and people experience healing. What an amazing opportunity we have to join our allegiance to the one government that will reign forever, putting all others to shame!

RELEVANT QUESTIONS

1. How does the call to kneel before a divine King differ from that of receiving a free gift of salvation to someday go to heaven?
2. Why does it matter that Jesus began and ended His ministry by preaching and teaching about the kingdom of God?
3. How is spiritual maturity affected when we do not preach and teach the kingdom?
4. What role should repentance play in the salvation process?

5. How does the kingdom of God differ from all earthly governments or kingdoms?
6. What hope-filled message can we draw from Daniel 2:44?
7. Why do our efforts to advance God's kingdom create conflict?
8. How can we create a kingdom culture in our lives and ministries?
9. Why is the state of our hearts important as we seek to advance God's kingdom on earth?
10. What happens when the kingdom of God visits earth?
11. What does it mean to be an ambassador for Christ?
12. Why should our witness for Christ hold a higher place within our hearts than our political affiliation?

CHAPTER FOURTEEN

OVERCOMING HINDRANCES TO PRAYER

Pastors routinely address the need for prayer, but I often wonder what role it actually plays in the life of the average church attender. Early Christians did not just pray; they championed a *culture of prayer*. And so it was that the early church became alive and vibrant, with miracles happening often.

Devout prayer seems to be less common in our day, and also more difficult. Christians will, of course, acknowledge the importance of prayer—even when they fail to cultivate a healthy and consistent prayer life. But all too often, prayer becomes the "last resort" in an attempt to remedy undesirable circumstances.

Drifting into prayerlessness opens the door for evil to thrive. The core of Christian living centers on a relationship with God (as opposed to religious duty or obligation), and prayer is integral to that relationship. Could you imagine a marriage relationship that focused on completing household tasks but lacked meaningful communication? Perhaps you can! If a meaningful prayer life is lacking, we can only fantasize about growing to spiritual maturity.

Because many excellent prayer resources have been created and many excellent sermons have been preached, I will use this brief space to identify some specific hindrances to prayer. By addressing these obstacles effectively, we can help people take meaningful steps in their relationship with God—and in the direction of spiritual maturity. Our goal is not to burden people's already strained shoulders with more expectations, but to release them into prayer by overcoming some of the hindrances.

1. **"I have no time to pray."** I remember a time during my campus ministry years when I knew I needed to pray more, but spent little focused time doing so. "I just don't have time to pray," I often lamented. Then, one day, I had a rare free block of time and could not decide what to do. The idea of praying entered my mind, and in that moment I had to admit that I did not feel inclined to pray. I had allowed a shortage of time to create a convenient excuse for my lack of desire.

   So, what do we tell those who feel they have no time to pray? "Get honest with yourself. And then get creative!" When Debi and I began dating many years ago, I learned quickly that we manage to make time for what we value. And while the ideal setting might be a personal "prayer closet" apart from the activity of everyday life, we can find other opportunities to draw near to the Lord. Praying while doing dishes is but one practical example of turning an otherwise mindless activity into a meaningful spiritual experience.

2. **"I do not have a good place to pray."** Life has its seasons—each of which carries different responsibilities and opportunities. Those who lack the privacy to pray in their current season of life can simply ask the Lord for guidance.

   Perhaps He will lead them to take a walk or visit a local park. Or maybe the Lord will open their eyes to another option. Susanna Wesley, the mother of John and Charles Wesley, would often throw her apron over her head during a busy day to commune with God. Despite the many demands she faced, the mother who gave birth to nineteen children found a way, and the world was changed!

3. **Distractions abound.** The rise of modern technology has created distractions unique to our day. Radio, TV, computers,

and cell phones often demand attention and can crowd out the times of quiet we need for effective prayer. If we do not cultivate discipline, our electronics will overrun our lives like invasive vines.

Modern electronics are so prevalent, and can have such a detrimental effect on our spiritual lives, that it is not beyond reason for church leaders to teach their people the disciplines of mastering digital communication devices. This approach assumes, of course, that pastors and church leaders are leading the way. For those who need improvement in this area, a personal step toward discipline might be the best place to start.

4. **People doubt God will answer their prayers because they do not grasp the nature of the gospel.**

   a. Some fail to believe His Word, and thus, His promises for answered prayer. We more naturally focus on negative circumstances than on the promises of God. That damaging tendency cannot be reversed if we do not believe in the credibility of the Bible. We can find plenty of excellent resources to teach people about the trustworthiness of the Christian Scriptures.

   b. They do not know His promises. If we do not regularly read God's Word, we will remain ignorant of the amazing promises within its pages. Instruction in daily Bible reading provides an excellent place to start.

   c. They feel inadequate. It is easy to feel insignificant even as a Christian—especially if we lack the public gifts of communication that enable leaders to rise to prominence. But God is no respecter of persons, and all believers have *equal* access to His throne of grace. Eloquence might impress other humans, but the Lord turns His ear toward humility and sincerity.

d. They feel unworthy because of a struggle with sin and guilt. People who are bound by sin, or burdened under the weight of guilt and condemnation, will hesitate to draw near to God in prayer. They mistakenly think they have to "clean up their act" before drawing near. Sometimes, the secret to helping a prayer life has more to do with the theology of grace than with prayer.

5. **People do not know what or how to pray.** Unfamiliar territory often feels uncomfortable. Sometimes, people need to learn to press through discomfort as part of the learning and growing process. Leaders can help overcome this barrier with teaching, meaningful opportunities, and a little nudging. There are many who want to take a forward step, but need help overcoming their fears.

   Throughout my years of ministry, I have been blessed with opportunities to nudge more than one devoted Christian into praying in public for the first time. I usually begin by asking about their desires. Is praying in public something they want to grow into? Then I ask permission to nudge them forward when I feel the time is appropriate. Finally, I encourage their efforts regardless of how feeble they might seem. If we exercise patience with those we serve, multiple little steps can lead to big changes!

6. **People have not learned to enjoy the presence of God.** All too often, we picture God the Father as a grumpy old man or a harsh judge. Those are the types of family members no one wants to visit. But some thoughtful reading of the Bible will open our eyes to the real God.

   > You will make known to me the path of life;
   > In Your presence is fullness of joy;
   > In Your right hand there are pleasures forever.
   > Psalm 16:11

How many people view prayer through the lens of enjoying God's presence? I think many of us have much to learn in this regard. Grasping the true nature of our Creator will help us grasp the true nature of prayer, which will draw us near like nothing else. And when we are near to the Lord, we are primed for growth!

THE BOTTOM LINE

The reasons for failing to pray are many, but prayer is so important and so powerful that the hindrances are worth addressing. Identifying the obstacles to vital prayer can help open people's eyes to the issues lurking beneath the surface of their lives. Better still, addressing those hindrances from the pulpit (or in a smaller group setting) can afford hesitant Christians the wisdom and strength to overcome every barrier.

RELEVANT QUESTIONS

1. On a scale of 1–10, how would you grade the prayer life of the American church?
2. How would you grade your own prayer life?
3. What were some keys to vibrant prayer in the early church?
4. What effect do you think modern technology has had on our individual prayer lives?
5. What are some creative ways you have learned to help better develop the discipline of prayer?
6. What advice would you give to a single parent of young children about finding a place to pray?
7. What is the single most effective thing you have done to make technology serve you instead of you serving technology?
8. How can a clear understanding of the Scriptures strengthen a person's prayer life?
9. How might a revelation of grace affect a person's prayer life?

10. What are some ways you have helped newer believers enhance their prayer lives?
11. Do you have any "secrets" for enjoying God's presence?

CHAPTER FIFTEEN

HONORING THE COVENANTS

Some of my readers likely employ a practice that irritates me greatly, but I guess we are far enough into this book that I can risk offending you. I am referring to the idea of creating church agreements and calling them "covenants" when they only faintly resemble the real thing.

The Western world has watered down the concept of covenant in modern times, and it is one of the reasons people struggle with trust. Our idea of a covenant resembles more of a contract, which does not carry the full weight of faithfulness embodied by the covenants of old.

COVENANTS DEFINED

Many students of God's Word recognize a covenant to be a *sacred and binding relationship*.[1] The nature of covenants might vary, but *faithfulness* and *trust* always stand as universal factors. Covenantal thinking characterized ancient treaties between people groups. And as we read through the Bible, we also see covenants established between individuals, such as the one between Jonathan and David. Most importantly, when God relates closely to humans, He does so through covenant relationships.

---

1. *Drinking Truth: Embracing the Covenant Mindset of the Bible* provides more detail about the ancient understanding of covenants and their modern applications.

What we call the Old and New "Testaments" are probably better described as the Old and New "Covenants." The word *testament* often flashes images of a last will and testament. It involves instructions a person expects others to follow *after* his or her death. But the Bible is far more than a book of instructions left by a since-departed God; it is a book of relationship, intended to bring us near to our Creator.

OUR WESTERN DRIFT

There was a day when covenantal thinking spanned our globe. A little historical research will reveal example after example of covenant relationships being established in varied places, such as Africa, Asia, and even at sea. The concept of "blood brotherhood" once had a far-reaching influence. Today's culture relegates covenantal thinking mainly to fantasy in books and movies.

Covenants are meant to deal in the realm of *absolute faithfulness*—a concept postmodern cultures struggle to grasp. Apart from some military groups and criminal gangs, there is not much in our modern world that mirrors covenantal thinking. Even the concept of marriage, which was once considered a prime example of a covenant relationship, has veered far from the foundations of sacred vows.

In the arena of covenants especially, relevance has its limitations. Rather than using substitute words such as "agreement" and "contract," we must educate our people on the meaning of covenants and their role in the Biblical story. Though we cannot find many modern examples for them to latch onto, the idea of God's unwavering faithfulness always resonates in human hearts.

TRUST IS SACRED

Covenants are sacred because trust is sacred. And trust is sacred because it forms the foundation for intimate relationships. In the ancient world, trust was so highly esteemed that those who established covenants often pronounced curses against anyone who might stoop low enough to break them. What strange ideas for modern societies in which the need of the moment rules over faithfulness to one's word!

Our drift from covenantal thinking also leaves us struggling to grasp the negative consequences of Adam and Eve's failure in Eden. The first three chapters of Genesis do not employ the word *covenant*, but scholars tell us covenant language is present. And it is within a covenantal context that the curses of Genesis 3 make sense. Without this context, those curses can appear as a huge overreaction on God's part.

God created Adam and Eve in His own image to enjoy a covenant relationship with Him. But by doubting the Lord and listening to the serpent, they violated a sacred trust and joined a cosmic coup attempt against the kingdom of heaven. Governments worldwide rightly regard treason as a crime worthy of death because it violates national trust, while aiding and abetting a hostile force.

For a person to become a naturalized citizen of the United States of America, he or she must take an *oath* of allegiance. This is a covenantal act that helps us better grasp the nature of the relationship between a government and its citizens. Because pride seeks to exalt itself against the throne of heaven, all humanity is guilty of treason against the greatest kingdom ever to exist.

CHANGES TO COVENANTS

When the Lord establishes a covenant, *only He* has the authority to change it (Galatians 3:15). And when God modifies a covenant, He will broadcast the new terms clearly. No human has the authority to change what God has ordained, and no amount of manipulation or jockeying for influence can change that.

The transition from the *Mosaic covenant of law* to the *new covenant of grace* serves as our classic example. Through His prophets, and then through Jesus and His apostles, the Lord announced a coming change (Jeremiah 31:31-34; Luke 22:20; Acts 10).

The *marriage covenant* that was established by God in Genesis 2:24 serves as a second covenant of record that remains relevant to our day.

> For this reason a man shall leave his father and his mother, and be joined to his wife; and they shall become one flesh. Genesis 2:24

In Old Testament times, the Lord often "looked the other way" regarding polygamy and divorce, but He never modified the original intent of the marriage covenant between one man and one woman. Why is this important? Rather than loosening the terms of the marriage covenant, Jesus called people back to God's original design (Matthew 19:3-12).

It is through a covenantal lens that Biblical prohibitions regarding sexual immorality become clear (Hebrews 13:4). We need not argue over the intended Greek meanings of New Testament words. Nor does it matter whether Jesus personally addressed issues such as homosexuality. *If God establishes a covenant for humanity, only God has the authority to change the terms.* And if the Lord does not enact an obvious change, no change is valid in the eyes of heaven.

The prevalence of divorce—even among Christians—complicates our discussion of these weighty issues. A thorough exploration of the topic would require more space than our format allows, but I want to encourage leaders to avoid two extremes regarding divorce. Jews in Jesus' day struggled to discern whether divorce should be allowed without cause, or only in extreme situations. In some ways, our current situation resembles theirs.

Not just Western culture, but even the Western church, has been too free and easy with divorce. Far too often, we view it as an unfortunate solution to problems that could be resolved with focused and humble effort. Divorce is never pain free, and it always causes collateral damage.

At the same time, we must remember that God made at least some provisions for divorce in both the Old and New Testaments. As much as marriage covenants should be unbreakable, human sinfulness complicates everything.

We miss the heart of God's intent if we do not exercise compassion toward those trapped in abusive situations. In particular, I see nothing Biblical about shunning a woman who divorces her husband to protect herself and her children from abuse. Vulnerable people in such difficult situations need our support and not our condemnation.

THE NEW COVENANT

The two primary sacraments of the Christian faith—*water baptism* and *communion*—are both rooted in covenantal thinking. How ironic that we so often celebrate the new covenant through communion when very few Westerners seem to grasp the nature of this sacred relationship!

Sadly, the evangelical church, of which I consider myself a part, often treats water baptism as an "add-on" to the salvation process. Water baptism, though, serves as our practical *initiation* into the new covenant. I do not believe baptism is necessary for salvation, but I am hard-pressed to find anywhere the early church treated it as an optional add-on to be considered at a person's discretion.

Our Western drift has caused us to "lower the bar," so to speak, in the salvation process. I do not encourage embracing legalism or compelling people to obey lists of rules. However, entry into a covenant relationship should never be taken lightly. At the very minimum, we should call a person to fully surrender his or her will to God as a primary expression of faith for salvation. Doing so can have a profound influence on the culture of a church because surrender both requires and precipitates a genuine change of heart. If we are not "all in" regarding the new covenant, we must question whether we are in at all.

THE BOTTOM LINE

Western culture has lost much because of its drift away from covenantal thinking. Unfortunately, the Western church has also drifted. If we want to help our people grow to spiritual maturity, we must regain our moorings by educating people to grasp both the nature and importance of covenantal thinking.

RELEVANT QUESTIONS

1. How would you define "covenant"?
2. What role does covenantal thinking play in the Bible?
3. How do contracts and covenants differ?
4. What are some examples of covenantal thinking that you see in society today?
5. How has the Western world watered down the concept of covenant?
6. How has a Western misunderstanding of covenant negatively influenced growth to maturity in the church?
7. What role did curses play in ancient covenants?
8. What do you think about the idea that trust is sacred?
9. Why is sexual immorality a covenantal issue?
10. What does Galatians 3:15 speak to you?
11. How do water baptism and communion reflect covenantal thinking?
12. How should covenantal thinking influence our preaching of the gospel?
13. What does it mean to be in covenant with God?

CHAPTER SIXTEEN

ESTABLISHING A SECURE IDENTITY

One of the greatest revelations God has given me for life and ministry centers on the importance of a *secure identity*.[1] And the more I have learned, the more I have realized how much this dynamic affects us all. In my early days of ministry, the Lord showed me how I had bundled my sense of identity with the pursuit of ministry success. Yes, I was seeking to advance God's kingdom on earth, but there was also a lot of *ME* in the mix. Little did I realize how a misplaced sense of identity undermined not only my spiritual health, but also my effectiveness in ministry.

CREATED FOR GLORY

Having formed us in His image, the Lord also created us for *glory*. But humans have no measure of significance within themselves apart from God. He alone is the source from whom all good things flow. So, when Adam and Eve ate from the forbidden tree, they separated themselves from divine glory. That is why they felt naked and ashamed after eating the forbidden fruit. If ever there was a divine spark within the human heart, it would have been extinguished the day Adam and Eve joined the cosmic rebellion.

Covering their exposed bodies with fig leaves seemed like the obvious solution to their plight, and all their descendants

---

1. *From Glory to Glory: Finding Real Significance in an Image-Driven World* provides more detailed insight into this vital topic.

continue to employ a similar approach. Instead of using real fig leaves, though, we use metaphorical ones. *Appearance, performance, possessions, position, knowledge,* and *association with others* are all means that we use in a vain attempt to cover our spiritual nakedness. But regardless of whether the fig leaves are real or symbolic, the outcome remains the same: we hide and isolate our true selves due to fear.

RIGHTEOUSNESS

The epic failure that unfolded in the shade of the tree of the knowledge of good and evil produced both *guilt* and *shame*, which leads us to realize that the concept of righteousness has both moral *and* social components. Moral, or *kingdom righteousness*, involves our ability to meet the love-based standards of the kingdom of heaven. *Social righteousness* involves our ability to measure up to the visible human standards of our subculture. Both forms of righteousness find their roots in law-based living. And while only the former directly affects eternal salvation, the latter still influences our ability to live in victory over sin.

Evangelical churches are full of people who understand their righteousness before God (kingdom righteousness) comes only through faith in the cross of Jesus Christ. But even devoted believers can still seek a sense of social righteousness by trying to measure up to the standards of their subcultures. How frequently they attend church, how much they give, and how long they pray can all become badges of honor that empower deadly pride. These precious souls might be saved and destined for heaven, but sadly, rotten fruit grows on many of the branches of their lives.

PRIDE AND CONFLICT

If we were to identify the most destructive problems of our day, division would be near the top of our list. What we rarely realize, though, is how much of our conflict stems from the root of pride. In particular, the quest to find a positive sense of identity within ourselves (apart from Christ) is killing our marriages, our churches, and our nations. If we consider the intensity and toxicity of the abounding conflicts in our political world, we come to realize more and more the futility of our human ways.

Diversity has always been a core component of the body of Christ, and so we need not force people into a path of conformity. But diverse people can get along only when their source of glory flows from Christ and not themselves. Otherwise, judgmental attitudes sprout and grow, exalting some on high pedestals, while pushing others into the dirt of social humiliation. It is in such an environment that the deceptiveness of a celebrity culture does its damage.

Trying to establish a flesh-based identity creates fault lines in our human experience, causing multiple problems both within and between us. We seek to view ourselves as superior and struggle to admit when we are wrong. Our insecurities also set us up for offense, propelling us into anger or panic any time someone threatens our sense of self-goodness.

An innate need for glory reaches to the heart of every person ever born, which means our pursuit of a favorable identity knows few bounds. And so it is that we display uncommon depths of emotion any time the "identity nerve" gets touched.

SONS AND DAUGHTERS OF GOD

Nothing is more personal than our identity, and few factors affect our behavior as much. It would make sense, then, for a loving God to address this vital issue. And He does—often more than we realize.

The gospel is not just a message of future destiny, but also of present identity. Through the cross of Christ, we become the honored and beloved children of God's Royal Family. And it is in sonship (a "generic" term including both males and females) that we find both our true identity and a deep sense of peace.

If we think about who God is—the highest and most glorious King ever to exist—being called "His child" is no trite matter. One day, the world will drool with envy for such a lofty status, but we need to grasp His profound favor now, by faith.

The story of Mephibosheth (2 Samuel 9) meshes well with Ephesians 2:1–10 to help us grasp this reality. The remainder of Ephesians 2 also provides powerful insight into how living by law for the sake of righteousness separates us. But walls of separation come crashing to the ground when we discover our source of righteousness—both kingdom and social—through the cross of Jesus Christ!

Because our identities are central to our existence, I return to the theme regularly. In doing so, I am not drawing from a well of modern-day psychology; I am plumbing the depths of God's Word to mine truths that were established long before humanity conceived of modern academic disciplines. The psychologists of today are merely discovering what has been true since the advent of time. And, more importantly, the gospel provides answers to our human condition in a way academia never can.

THE BOTTOM LINE

We naturally draw our sense of significance from both self-effort and the approval of others. But this approach finds its roots in the prideful hiss of the serpent that beguiled Adam and Eve long ago. God's design, and the one through which true freedom reigns, is for us to realize our esteemed identity as the beloved children of heaven's Royal Family. All that we do then flows from that innate sense of security. And the fruit is marvelous!

RELEVANT QUESTIONS

1. What is the significance of being created in the image of God?
2. In what way is identity about glory?

3. How do you define glory?
4. What happens when people experience a loss of glory?
5. What symbolic fig leaves do you see being used in the world today? How about in the church?
6. How would you describe the difference between kingdom and social righteousness?
7. How can pride create conflict?
8. How do judgmental attitudes relate to identity?
9. How has a "celebrity culture" damaged the mission of the church?
10. In what ways is the gospel a message of identity?
11. Why is sonship the highest form of identity?
12. What is the significance of being a child of God?
13. What happens when we draw our sense of significance from our ministry efforts rather than from our relationship with the Lord?
14. What powerful lessons can we glean from the story of Mephibosheth found in 2 Samuel 9?

CHAPTER SEVENTEEN

PULLING DOWN IDOLS

When Adam and Eve chose to trust the serpent over God, they embraced multiple lies and half-truths. Some were obvious, others not so much. One of the more subtle lies suggested that God and His provision were not enough; they needed something more. It is from this lie that the poisonous root of *idolatry* sprouts.

The Lord created us in His image with the capacity to rule over the created order. When we align with God and yield to His authority, we are empowered to exercise stewardship effectively. But if we fail to align with His ways, we become subjects—instead of rulers—of that created order. Idolatry soon prevails.

Promising a better tomorrow, idols become the focus of worship, blessing, and trust. In ancient times (and in some cultures today), physical representations of wood, silver, and gold were created to depict supposed gods. The form might be different in modern advanced cultures, but idols continue to exist because demonic spirits use them to garner attention and draw people's attention away from the one true God.

> No, but I say that the things which the Gentiles sacrifice, they sacrifice to demons and not to God; and I do not want you to become sharers in demons. You cannot drink the cup of the Lord and the cup of demons; you cannot partake of the table of the Lord and the table of demons. 1 Corinthians 10:20–21

Because demonic spirits drive idolatry, they use their dark influence to torment and destroy—not bless—human lives. To make matters worse, the Lord never takes kindly to the worship of imposter gods. If you want to understand why He sent ancient Israel into Babylonian exile, consider their idolatrous practices.

SPIRITUAL ADULTERY

The worship of false gods served as perhaps the most significant factor in the demise of ancient Israel. The Lord likened idolatry to adultery, as though His bride was going after other lovers (Hosea 4). And it was not just other lovers, but bad actors who would leave the people of Israel wallowing in misery. Idols are always abusive masters.

People naturally walk by sight instead of faith, which means that idolatry has been common throughout history. Virtually every ancient civilization had its own set of deities. Skilled craftsmen produced handcrafted statues and massive, ornate temples to appease their supposed gods. And those efforts sometimes included not only ritual prostitution, but also human sacrifice.

Despite many, many warnings sent by God through His prophets, the people of Israel persisted in idol worship. The sad result was a nation destroyed and dragged into captivity. Because the people of ancient Israel abandoned God to worship idols, He abandoned them to captivity, destruction, and death—but not entirely. Even throughout their exile, the Lord's promises for a blessed future remained (Jeremiah 29:11–13).

After exile in Babylon, the light began to dawn on the nation of Israel. They woke up and abandoned their idols, but only in a sense. Often, idolatry simply took other forms.

Idolatry continues to be common in our day, though its expressions are often more subtle than those in ancient cultures. Besides the literal idols worshiped in nations across the globe, people also serve the gods of:

- Money and materialism
- Romantic partners and family members
- Music, film, and athletic superstars
- Entertainment
- Politicians
- Hobbies
- Ministry and ministers

Most of the items on this list are not inherently bad; it is the unhealthy place they hold in human hearts that creates problems.

Anything we put in the place of God becomes an idol, and none of them can satisfy our deep-rooted needs the way He can. Even good things like Christian ministry can become idolatrous if they replace the Lord as our *First Love*. This is made evident through the celebrity mindset that has wreaked havoc within Christian circles, damaging lives and hindering the cause of the gospel. Ministers are called to humbly care for and equip people for service—not stand aloof as star personalities to whom "common folk" can never attain.

MISPLACED TRUST

At the heart of idolatry lies the sin of *misplaced trust*. Certainly, we need to trust one another, but ultimately, there is only one God from whom we have our being. He alone has the power to restore, provide, and guide. When we direct the trust we owe God to other sources, we pollute the waters of our lives.

> Thus says the Lord,
> "Cursed is the man who trusts in mankind
> And makes flesh his strength,
> And whose heart turns away from the Lord.

> For he will be like a bush in the desert
> And will not see when prosperity comes,
> But will live in stony wastes in the wilderness,
> A land of salt without inhabitant."
> Jeremiah 17:5–6

What irony! As it was with eating from the tree of the knowledge of good and evil, elevating idols has the opposite of its intended effect. People look to idolatrous means in pursuit of blessings, provision, and vitality. They instead receive a stony wasteland. This is how the deceptive wiles of the devil work as they entice us to follow decaying paths in search of fulfillment.

As bad as this all sounds, the next two verses in Jeremiah paint a bright picture of healthy spirituality:

> "Blessed is the man who trusts in the Lord
> And whose trust is the Lord.
> For he will be like a tree planted by the water,
> That extends its roots by a stream
> And will not fear when the heat comes;
> But its leaves will be green,
> And it will not be anxious in a year of drought
> Nor cease to yield fruit."
> Jeremiah 17:7–8

Genuine trust yields life-giving blessings. *The Lord will sometimes lead us through dry wilderness territory, but He never wants us to be dry within ourselves.*[1] If we feel spiritually parched, the root problem is likely misplaced trust, often in the form of idolatry.

As with the people of old, God continues to warn His children about the dangers of idolatry. Still, He will allow us to linger in a barren spiritual wilderness while calling us back to Biblical faith and pure worship. Experiencing the symptoms of spiritual barrenness should compel us to search for the root cause(s)

---

1. My *Champions in the Wilderness* devotional expounds upon this dynamic in greater detail, providing strength and encouragement, along with timely instruction.

involved. So often, the path to healthy spirituality involves identifying our idols, turning away from their destructive influence, and cultivating trust in the only true Savior.

People naturally worship and serve idols, so we will always face pressure to embrace the gods of human culture. Ancient Jews and Christians suffered persecution because of their refusal to bow down to false gods, and those pressures remain today. Yes, pure worship comes at a price, but the cost of serving a false god is far greater.

THE BOTTOM LINE

Idolatry is not just a primitive practice of the past. Dark spirits continue to draw people away from an abiding relationship with the Giver of Life. By exposing misplaced trust and calling people back to pure worship, we can help them cultivate an abiding relationship that bears sweet and lasting fruit.

RELEVANT QUESTIONS

1. In what does idolatry have its roots?
2. Why is idolatry so common?
3. What makes an idol deceptive?
4. Why are idols bad masters?
5. Why does God take offense to idolatry?
6. In what way does idolatry equate to adultery?
7. How can each of the following become an idol?
    a. Money and materialism
    b. Romantic partners and family members
    c. Superstars
    d. Politicians
    e. Hobbies

    f. Entertainment

    g. Ministry and ministers

8. How do we know when we have crossed a line from spiritual health into idolatry?

9. What is the problem with misplaced trust? (Jeremiah 17:5–6)

10. Please read Jeremiah 17:7–8. What are the benefits of focusing our trust on God?

11. In what ways are Christians pressured to adhere to false gods?

12. What damage can a celebrity mindset inflict upon the cause of the gospel?

13. What are the key steps to breaking free from idolatry?

CHAPTER EIGHTEEN

SEVERING THE EVIL ROOT

Jesus spoke on many topics. Traveling through town and country, He taught about love and faith and the power of God. But there was one subject Jesus seemed to broach more than any other: money and materialism. Much of the time, our Lord used money and materialism to illustrate kingdom concepts. But He also spoke strongly about the place these things hold in human hearts.

Why would this be? Why would the Son of God, who brought heaven to earth, spend so much time addressing such a seemingly mundane topic? As a masterful teacher, the Lord illuminated unseen spiritual concepts using examples from everyday life. But that is not all. As is typical with God, there is also more to the story.

THE IDOL OF MATERIALISM

Worldly wealth is one of the most enduring idols to which people bend their knee. And it is probably the most prevalent source of misplaced trust known to humanity. We live in a material world, and wealth captures our hearts with its many promises. In worldly wealth we place our confidence for tomorrow, grasping for security amid uncertainty. And while we focus on what money can do *for us*, Jesus wisely addressed what money can do *to us*.

> "Do not store up for yourselves treasures on earth, where moth and rust destroy, and where thieves break in and steal. But store up for yourselves treasures in heaven, where neither moth nor rust destroys, and where thieves do not break in or steal; for where your treasure is, there your heart will be also. . . . No one can serve two masters; for either he will hate the one and love the other, or he will be devoted to one and despise the other. You cannot serve God and wealth." Matthew 6:19–21, 24

The original Greek language of this passage uses the term *mamōnás* for wealth. According to the *Theological Dictionary of the New Testament*:

> The Gk. *mamōnás* seems to come from an Aramaic noun which most probably derives from the root *'mn* ("that in which one trusts").[1]

This explanation makes sense. Wealth reaches far, and its influence runs deep—to the point of enslaving us. Just think about some things that people do to fill their pockets. Lying, stealing, and even killing have been common means that greedy people throughout history have used to grab material wealth. Even Christians must deal daily with issues of food and provision, if not the temptation for excessive material gain.

Poverty leads to a pain-filled existence, while material wealth promises happiness like nothing else. But just as the allure of sex far surpasses our need within a marriage relationship, so too, the attraction of wealth reaches beyond our need for material provision. In the end, we either use money or money uses us. The idea runs against our natural logic, but those who embrace materialism become slaves to that which they assume to master.

---

1. Gerhard Kittel, Gerhard Friedrich, and Geoffrey William Bromiley, *Theological Dictionary of the New Testament: Abridged in One Volume* (Grand Rapids, MI: W.B. Eerdmans, 1985), 552.

If we want to see people grow and thrive, money must be one of the friction-point topics we address—but not just to motivate Christians to give. I have heard plenty of pastors preach to their people about the blessings of material wealth—usually in the context of soliciting funds—but painfully few address the dangers laid out in Scripture.

> But those who want to get rich fall into temptation and a snare and many foolish and harmful desires which plunge men into ruin and destruction. For the love of money is a root of all sorts of evil, and some by longing for it have wandered away from the faith and pierced themselves with many griefs. 1 Timothy 6:9–10

Wow! Paul's message is not comfortable, but it is vital. When it comes to spiritual dangers, the allure of material riches must be near the top of the list! Material greed imprisons, while the pursuit of true wealth—wisdom—frees us.

TRUTHS ABOUT MONEY AND MATERIALISM

Human eyes usually open to the vanity of wealth at the time of death, but by then life's opportunities are past. Spiritual leaders and guides have a sacred responsibility to accurately address the dynamics of materialism while people still have an opportunity to make changes. Allow me to highlight several specific truths:

- **Money is a resource, nothing more.** Jesus called wealth "unrighteous" because of the negative influence it so often has on people (Luke 16:9). But wealth can also be used for good. The difference lies in how we see and use it. Wisdom calls us to use money as a *resource* to care for needs and advance the kingdom of God on earth.

- **We are stewards and not owners.** The Lord owns the earth and all that is in it, but He has entrusted this planet to us as His *stewards* (Psalm 115:16). We are not owners but managers of God's resources—and one day we will give an account of how we handled our Master's possessions.

- **People mistakenly treat material wealth as a badge of honor.** The more they have, the more elite they feel. And, of course, society promotes this mindset on just about every level. It is all a lie, though, creating a false sense of significance that blinds us to spiritual nakedness. Jesus' letter to the Laodicean church illustrates this truth painfully well (Revelation 3:14–22).

- **Money gives a false sense of security.** Even Christians can fail to recognize the temporal nature of this world's possessions. Those who place the weight of their trust on worldly wealth will see it abandon them when they need help most.

  > The name of the Lord is a strong tower;
  > The righteous runs into it and is safe.
  > A rich man's wealth is his strong city,
  > And like a high wall in his own imagination.
  > Proverbs 18:10–11

  > Do not weary yourself to gain wealth,
  > Cease from your consideration of it.
  > When you set your eyes on it, it is gone.
  > For wealth certainly makes itself wings
  > Like an eagle that flies toward the heavens.
  > Proverbs 23:4–5

- **Those preoccupied with material wealth will forfeit the inheritance of true riches that come through Christ.** Not only will they fail to accumulate treasures in heaven, they will also miss the wealth of spiritual wisdom flowing from heaven's throne (Colossians 2:1–4).

- **Money tests us.** We can tell how much God values material wealth by observing whom He allows to accumulate it. The Lord *seemingly* looks the other way while people obtain riches by selfish and unjust means, but His watchful eye misses nothing. One day, the test will be over, and the results displayed for all to see (Luke 12:13–21).

- **Misplaced trust is a primary cause of spiritual dryness and malaise (Jeremiah 17:5–6).** The financially prosperous are especially at risk because faith flourishes only as we exercise it. Comfortable people will struggle to keep their faith vibrant, if they keep it alive at all. As terrible as something like high inflation might be, atrophied faith has far worse consequences.

Because people's perspectives regarding money influence their spiritual well-being so deeply, a wise and caring leader will address the topic routinely. Furthermore, there should be times when we teach about materialism *apart from* making financial appeals. This approach will bring people face to face with the state of their hearts by removing any excuse to discount the message preached.

THE BOTTOM LINE

I have provided only a sampling of the many facets of spirituality related to material wealth. If spiritual maturity is the goal, putting material goods in their proper place is necessary.

RELEVANT QUESTIONS

1. In what ways can worldly wealth become an idol?
2. Please read Matthew 6:19–24. What does Jesus' statement "You cannot serve God and wealth" mean to you?
3. How does material wealth enslave people?

4. What are some of the more extreme things you have seen people do for money?
5. What are some pains you have seen people bring upon themselves through greed?
6. Why should we see money as no more than a resource or tool?
7. What does it mean to say that we are stewards and not owners of material resources?
8. Why did Jesus call wealth "unrighteous" in Luke 16:9?
9. What happens when people view wealth as a badge of honor?
10. Please comment on Proverbs 18:10–11 and Proverbs 23:4–5.
11. How can a preoccupation with worldly wealth cause people to forfeit their true inheritance in Christ?
12. In what ways does money test us?
13. How can pastors talk about money and materialism without appearing greedy?

Section Four

Solidifying the Distinctives of Maturity

- Preserving the Unity of the Faith
- Learning to Resolve Conflict Well
- Dealing with Counterfeit Leaders
- Caring for Ourselves
- Glorifying God
- Cultivating Faithfulness

Until I come, give attention to the public reading of Scripture, to exhortation and teaching. Do not neglect the spiritual gift within you, which was bestowed on you through prophetic utterance with the laying on of hands by the presbytery. Take pains with these things; be absorbed in them, so that your progress will be evident to all. Pay close attention to yourself and to your teaching; persevere in these things, for as you do this you will ensure salvation both for yourself and for those who hear you.

1 Timothy 4:13–16

CHAPTER NINETEEN

PRESERVING THE UNITY OF THE FAITH

Of all the topics related to spiritual maturity, unity stands out as one of the most challenging to address.[1] Unity provides both a path to, and a marker for, maturity. The apostle Paul frequently appealed for unity in his letters, and only a unified church will build itself up in love (Ephesians 4:16).

Pastors commonly preach about unity within their churches, but we must also consider a broader perspective. Of course, the principles of unity apply within the local church, but the issues we face also transcend any single church or community.

THE COVENANT BODY OF CHRIST

In addressing Christian unity, I am not referring to a humanly constructed *uniformity* that disregards the diversity of Christ's body. The Lord is building His people together as "living stones," not pressed bricks (1 Peter 2:4–5).

Our Christian unity is *covenantal*, being rooted in the person of Jesus Christ. If you enter a covenant relationship with Christ, and I enter a covenant relationship with Christ, by God's design, we join in covenant with one another. We truly are *brothers* and *sisters* in the highest sense. And our heavenly Father expects us to act like it. Always, our goal is to edify—to build others up instead of following the world's pattern of tearing down.

---

1. *Greater Glory: The Transformational Power of Christian Unity* is designed to help us navigate this challenging topic.

We are not attempting to create unity. Instead, through love, we faithfully *preserve* what God has *already* created through the new covenant (Ephesians 4:1–13). The Scriptures leave no wiggle room for excuses. In almost every one of his church letters, the apostle Paul appealed for Christian unity because he knew well the ramifications.

The problem with living stones is that they have rough edges. Sadly, many of us have become adept at justifying our failure to love and esteem fellow members of Christ's body. We somehow feel that different doctrines, practices, and styles give us license to criticize and condemn. Yes, we have differences, but our common ground through Jesus far outweighs them all.

Valuing unity does not mean we must ignore false doctrines and unhealthy practices, but our Lord does call us to address such issues with pure motives and humble hearts (Galatians 6:1). Jesus established a new standard by calling His followers to love even their enemies (Matthew 5:43–45). If God calls us to love our enemies, how much more should we love our brothers and sisters in the faith?

FOUR REASONS UNITY MATTERS

The importance of unity is widely recognized but not always embraced. From a Christian perspective, I can think of at least four reasons unity deserves more of our attention.

1. **Unity strengthens, while division weakens.** This is a universal truth. In Genesis 11, we read the story of the Tower of Babel. If God's enemies could have so much potential in their unity, how much more can His own people accomplish?

    Jesus also spoke candidly about the negative consequences of disunity:

    > "Any kingdom divided against itself is laid waste; and any city or house divided against itself will not stand."
    > Matthew 12:25b

If we consider how much cultural influence the church has lost over the past several decades, we can identify many reasons. Perhaps one of the most damaging involves the deep divisions marring the body of Christ. There have been times throughout history when the church was a nation's most powerful cultural influence, but we have squandered much of that because of spiritual immaturity and our inability to get along.

2. **We alienate young people when we are divided.** Christianity presents a high ideal by calling us to love even our enemies. We teach that ideal to our children, only to send a conflicting message when we treat fellow Christians with contempt and disdain. Young people are not blind to hypocrisy and they naturally recoil. If we want them to embrace the Christian faith, our words and actions must align with our message.

3. **We alienate the unsaved when we are divided.** Jesus made several powerful statements in the last hours before He went to the cross. One, in particular, often goes ignored:

> "A new commandment I give to you, that you love one another, even as I have loved you, that you also love one another. By this all men will know that you are My disciples, if you have love for one another." John 13:34–35

Through these words, Jesus gave people the right to judge the depth of our devotion based on our treatment of other Christians. A cross necklace means nothing if we do not love and respect our brothers and sisters in Christ.

4. **Our Lord passionately desires our unity.** Why do we do what we do? What defines our Christian experience? A deep and sincere love for God should be the biggest motivating factor in our lives (Revelation 2:1–7). If we truly love Him, we will value what He values. And Jesus' High Priestly Prayer opens our eyes to God's passions:

> "I do not ask on behalf of these alone, but for those also who believe in Me through their word; that they may all be one; even as You, Father, are in Me and I in You, that they also may be in Us, so that the world may believe that You sent Me.
>
> "The glory which You have given Me I have given to them, that they may be one, just as We are one; I in them and You in Me, that they may be perfected in unity, so that the world may know that You sent Me, and loved them, even as You have loved Me." John 17:20–23

Note Jesus' use of repetition (see also John 17:11) in this vital prayer. No good parent wants to see a family divided, and our heavenly Father is no different. God delights when His people are unified in love. How much do our Lord's desires mean to us? If we truly love Him, we will make unity a priority.

THE LAST DAYS' CHURCH

Sometimes, the church seems like a lost cause. Far too many leaders have succumbed to the lures of pride, power, and lust. And far too many congregants have wallowed in fleshly living. But our God is doing a powerful work in these last days as He raises up a bride without spot or blemish (Ephesians 5:25–27). A vital part of the process involves Christians from various streams loving and serving together with one heart through one Spirit.

One of the greatest triumphs for the people of God involves honoring and esteeming one another in love, while the world descends into conflict and turmoil. Indeed, our unity is a primary means through which God reveals His glory to people who are desperate for hope.

On a personal level, isolation undermines the vitality and effectiveness of a Christian leader. We need one another if we are to navigate well the tumultuous waters of ministry in today's world. And on a broader level, we need each other to maximize the effectiveness of our ministry efforts. The church functions far more effectively as a body than as a group of isolated pieces.

The process is not perfect—no endeavor involving humanity can be—but the walls are falling as God's people realize they are all members of one body. In communities large and small, Christian leaders are meeting for fellowship and prayer. I have been involved in such efforts and they renew and refresh my soul in an era when so much drains our vitality.

Our communities need a unified church to come together in prayer. Far too many souls are going to the grave without an accurate knowledge of our Savior. When the people of God pray with one voice, heaven imparts a rich blessing of *life* to those dwelling on earth.

> Behold, how good and how pleasant it is
> For brothers to dwell together in unity!
> It is like the precious oil upon the head,
> Coming down upon the beard,
> Even Aaron's beard,
> Coming down upon the edge of his robes.
> It is like the dew of Hermon
> Coming down upon the mountains of Zion;
> For there the Lord commanded the blessing—life forever.
> Psalm 133

Recognizing the relationship between love, unity, and life, I close this chapter by asking: Do you love the Lord enough to endure the shortcomings of other members of His family? What diligent steps are you taking to preserve the unity of the Spirit in the bond of peace? How are you relating to other Christians in your community? What can you do to encourage, strengthen, and bless them? Making such efforts will challenge you, but the opportunities to bless our Savior and the souls for whom He died are endless!

THE BOTTOM LINE

God has a powerful plan for our day, and the unity of His church remains central to that plan. Of course, individual churches can make a significant difference, but only *together* can we bring community transformation to the degree it is needed.

Love makes unity a reality. God loved us first, and we love Him in return. Those who truly love the Lord will also love those whom He loves. We do not need a theology degree to grasp these ideas, but we do need a passionate love for our Savior to live them out.

RELEVANT QUESTIONS

1. What is the difference between unity and uniformity?
2. In what way is Christian unity covenantal?
3. Why is the call to unity an admonition to walk in love?
4. What are some ways we build up or tear down others?
5. What excuses do we use to justify failing to love our brothers and sisters in Christ?
6. Discuss each of the following:
    a. Unity strengthens, while division weakens.
    b. We alienate young people when we are divided.
    c. We alienate the unsaved when we are divided.
    d. Our Lord passionately desires our unity.
7. How does Christian unity reveal the glory of God?
8. In what ways do you see walls of separation falling among Christians?
9. What are your thoughts about Psalm 133?
10. What are some practical steps your church can take to bring down the walls that separate God's people?

CHAPTER TWENTY

LEARNING TO RESOLVE CONFLICT WELL

It would not be an overstatement to say that our world has a colossal problem with conflict and division. The challenge is not just that we are divided, but that so many people are divisive. Start a social media thread about any public topic, and it will likely degrade into accusations, criticisms, and insults after only a handful of posts.

Part of the problem is unique to our era. The internet provides an opportunity to criticize from afar that few people would have ever dared when face to face. Not surprisingly, money also factors into the mix. Controversy and rage generate clicks, which creates advertising revenue. Activists also use outrage as a tool to raise money and facilitate changes that conform to their agendas. Finally, some forces disrupt intentionally. Bitter people take delight in creating conflict, while foreign entities seed division in their efforts to weaken a nation. And how easily we have played into their nefarious hands!

Our problem with conflict resembles the plague of illicit drugs that has destroyed so many lives. Remove the demand, and the market would crumble. In other words, division takes root because people repeatedly fall prey to divisive efforts. And if we were to pull back a spiritual curtain, we would see dark forces at work behind the scenes. Dividing Christians is one of the most effective ways to stall the advancement of God's kingdom on earth.

Children often live what they see modeled, which means the breakdown of the nuclear family leads to younger generations lacking the skills to resolve conflict effectively. Furthermore, because a vast number of people also struggle with insecurity, they tend to avoid uncomfortable discussions. Why go through the discomfort of working through a disagreement in person when you can send off a barrage of angry texts?

Conflict resolution is a learned skill. Parents, pastors, and church leaders should know they can play an enormous role in helping equip younger believers. In this very practical way, leaders can help the church to more effectively advance God's kingdom amid humanity.

The following ten steps do not present a comprehensive plan to resolve every conflict, but they do provide a helpful starting point for teaching people how to work through disagreements in a healthy way.[1]

Ten Steps of Conflict Resolution

1. **Seek to understand our heavenly Father's perspective.** Getting God's vantage point is one of the best ways to begin resolving a conflict. The great Judge of the universe is not partial (Romans 2:11). Righteousness and justice form the foundation of His throne (Psalm 89:14). God is like an *objective* parent who can discern a situation without the emotional biases that so often cloud our judgment. "Lord, please open my eyes to Your perspective," is an excellent prayer to help begin the process. Reading the book of Proverbs routinely will also help.

2. **Honor the covenants.** Covenant relationships are sacred in heaven's eyes. So why do we often treat worst those whom we should honor most? Is it because we are familiar with them? Do we lack gratitude? Or do we thoughtlessly react out of our pain?

---

1. These ten steps are taken from chapter 8 of *Greater Glory: The Transformational Power of Christian Unity*.

Seeking to honor a covenant relationship will not eliminate every source of conflict, but it will help create an environment that makes favorable resolutions more likely.

3. **Search your heart and contemplate your motives.** Self-reflection can be a powerful tool for conflict resolution. We naturally want to extend blame, but an objective look at our motives and emotions helps to enlarge our perspective. "Why was I offended?" "Why am I angry?" "What is hindering me from wanting to reconcile?" By better understanding ourselves, we become better equipped to work through difficult situations.

4. **Choose to obey God's command to forgive (Matthew 18:21–22).** Our willingness to forgive should never depend on another person's response. Letting go of bitterness not only helps clear our vision, but it also enables us to speak with grace. Forgiveness is a choice, and those who refuse to let go of bitterness will play into the devil's destructive hands.

5. **Extinguish fires while they are small.** In dry times, even a small spark can create a massive blaze. If you want to avoid unnecessary drama and exhausting conflicts, deal with issues while they are small—before they get out of control.

    Something similar applies to gossip, which acts like dry wood in the fires of conflict. A few select questions should be asked before sharing a sensitive matter with another person. "Have I spoken with the offending individual first?" "Will this conversation bring healing or further division?" "Am I looking for a solution or just someone to agree with me?"

6. **Invite God into the situation through prayer.** The Lord works when we yield control to Him. And in many ways, that is what prayer is all about. Praying involves yielding to heaven's King, crying out to Him for wisdom, and taking authority over dark spiritual forces. Prayer will not override another person's will,

but it does create an environment for hearts to soften and difficult situations to resolve.

7. **Choose an effective method of communication and use it.** Each situation is unique, and we want to prayerfully determine both the timing and method for effective communication. Meeting face to face is usually the most effective way to resolve an issue, but not always. Regardless of the method, though, avoidance usually makes matters worse.

8. **Seek to understand the other person's perspective.** When we genuinely try to understand another person's viewpoint, we open the door for discussion and might come away surprised by what we discover. Sometimes, we can avoid conflict simply by asking nonthreatening questions instead of lashing out with accusations. We might also spare ourselves the added pain that comes with making a false accusation.

9. **Speak truthfully, but graciously.** Proverbs 15:1 tells us, "A gentle answer turns away wrath, but a harsh word stirs up anger." How difficult it is to resolve conflict when we strive to prove ourselves right, or seek to put another person in his or her place! If reconciliation is our goal, speaking harshly will only work against us.

10. **Follow through.** If you make a promise or commitment in the process of resolving a conflict, do what you said you would do. Healthy relationships require trust, and failing to follow through is one of the quickest ways to destroy any progress made. Following through also means refusing to allow bitterness to worm its way back into your heart.

In an ideal world, we would be happy with the outcome of every attempt to resolve conflict. Reality, however, often differs. We cannot control the attitudes, words, or actions of others. And if a person is prone to rage or violence, seeking wise counsel might be necessary.

As long as we honor the Lord by doing our best to resolve the conflict, we can be at peace and trust Him for the rest. Regardless of how other people respond, we always want to be peacemakers at heart.

> "Blessed are the peacemakers, for they shall be called sons of God." Matthew 5:9

Finally, we must avoid looking at conflict resolution skills in static terms. One situation does not permanently label a person. Life will provide plenty of opportunities to learn and practice the skills needed for healthy conflict resolution. Part of growing to spiritual maturity involves learning from each situation regardless of whether we experience failure or success.

THE BOTTOM LINE

The ability to successfully resolve conflict is a learned skill requiring humility and dependence upon God. And while there is no guarantee that every situation will work out as we hope, following the ten basic steps of conflict resolution will take a Christian a long way in the learning process.

RELEVANT QUESTIONS

1. How prevalent is conflict in our day compared to times past?
2. How have conflict and disunity affected your efforts to serve and lead others?
3. What are some causes of disunity in our nation? How about in the church?
4. What are some things pastors and church leaders can do to help their people develop skills for effective conflict resolution?
5. Discuss the dynamics of each of the following steps to resolving conflict:

a. Seek to understand our heavenly Father's perspective.
   b. Honor the covenants.
   c. Search your heart and contemplate your motives.
   d. Choose to forgive.
   e. Extinguish fires while they are small.
   f. Invite God into the situation through prayer.
   g. Choose an effective means of communication and use it.
   h. Seek to understand the other person's perspective.
   i. Speak truthfully, but graciously.
   j. Follow through.
6. Why is it unrealistic to expect every effort toward conflict resolution to work out perfectly?
7. Why is it vital to have a growth mindset regarding conflict resolution skills?

CHAPTER TWENTY-ONE

DEALING WITH COUNTERFEIT LEADERS

I doubt you have ever been to the United States of Kailasa. It is a "borderless, service-oriented country" that once boasted of a special "sister-city" relationship with Newark, NJ, along with several other US cities.[1]

Kailasa was created by the "Supreme Pontiff of Hinduism" (SPH), Paramahamsa Nithyananda, and "established on the principle of Oneness" as "the first sovereign state for Hindus."

Nithyananda claims Kailasa to be a small island off the coast of Ecuador. But despite issuing passports and creating its own monetary system, the nation has no international recognition. Ecuador does not even acknowledge its existence. Furthermore, the SPH is a fugitive from justice in India for rape and child abduction. His followers would disagree, but many widely regard Paramahamsa Nithyananda as a cult leader.

For a short time, Kailasa established a special "sister-city" status with the city of Newark, NJ. It also received special recognition by about thirty other cities and even a couple members of the US Congress. Much of this took place because several female "ambassadors" of Kailasa made focused efforts to establish connections out of devotion to their Supreme Pontiff.

For some reason, public officials failed—or were afraid—to ask reasonable questions of noble-sounding representatives. And

---

1. Michael Kaplan, "Inside the 'Cult' That Fooled Newark into Being Sister Cities with a Fake Nation," *New York Post*, March 21, 2023, accessed January 26, 2024, https://nypost.com/2023/03/21/inside-cult-that-fooled-newark-nj-with-fake-sister-city/.

so they were duped into complicity by outward appearances. The story might seem bizarre, but it is not entirely unique. All throughout history, people have been convinced to embrace false realities.

WARNINGS ABOUT FALSE PROPHETS

Appearances often betray reality, which is why it is dangerous to avoid the topic of false prophets. Scripture contains strong warnings about their influence, and we would do well to take heed. Jesus made the first New Testament mention of false prophets, and His words are some of the most frightening in Scripture:

> "Beware of the false prophets, who come to you in sheep's clothing, but inwardly are ravenous wolves. You will know them by their fruits. Grapes are not gathered from thorn bushes nor figs from thistles, are they? So every good tree bears good fruit, but the bad tree bears bad fruit. A good tree cannot produce bad fruit, nor can a bad tree produce good fruit. Every tree that does not bear good fruit is cut down and thrown into the fire. So then, you will know them by their fruits.
>
> "Not everyone who says to Me, 'Lord, Lord,' will enter the kingdom of heaven, but he who does the will of My Father who is in heaven will enter. Many will say to Me on that day, 'Lord, Lord, did we not prophesy in Your name, and in Your name cast out demons, and in Your name perform many miracles?' And then I will declare to them, 'I never knew you; depart from Me, you who practice lawlessness.'" Matthew 7:15–23

Some leaders claim Jesus was speaking against the use of spiritual gifts after the early church era, but that perspective does not fit the overall context of the Scriptures. Instead, the Son of God made a powerful point using what some believe to be the most spiritual aspects of dynamic ministry.

As significant as they might be, it is not miraculous signs that indicate a close relationship with God, but rather the presence of *good spiritual fruit* (Galatians 5:22–23). This fruit, as we know from John 15:1–8, is the indicator of an *abiding relationship* with God. So when people look to identify with spiritual leaders, the existence—or lack—of good fruit should be a primary consideration.

The apostle Paul also spoke to the elders of Ephesus about counterfeit leaders, and his words were just as disturbing as our Lord's:

> "Be on guard for yourselves and for all the flock, among which the Holy Spirit has made you overseers, to shepherd the church of God which He purchased with His own blood. I know that after my departure savage wolves will come in among you, not sparing the flock; and from among your own selves men will arise, speaking perverse things, to draw away the disciples after them. Therefore be on the alert, remembering that night and day for a period of three years I did not cease to admonish each one with tears." Acts 20:28–31

For three years, Paul warned the believers in Ephesus about the danger of false prophets. And some deceivers would come from among their own number. But mature Christians will not be duped!

A mark of spiritual maturity, according to Paul, is that people are no longer "children, tossed here and there by waves and carried about by every wind of doctrine, by the trickery of men, by craftiness in deceitful scheming" (Ephesians 4:14b).

Just as the serpent's smooth words enticed Adam and Eve under the shadow of the forbidden tree, counterfeit leaders profess the ways of God while living according to their fleshly desires. Even noble-sounding words, we must realize, can present an appealing pathway to dungeons of death.

DECEPTIVE WORDS

What is it that makes the messages of false prophets so deceptive? More often than not, a false prophet proclaims something we desire to be true. Because we want to find significance, meaning, love, money, etc., it is easy to embrace smooth words promising to fulfill these innate desires. And make no mistake, we must all be on guard.

Effective Christian ministry does not just compel people to believe in God and act accordingly; it also trains them to pursue and discern truth (Hebrews 5:11–14). And while emotions can play a vital role in our devotion to the Lord, a faith built upon feelings creates dangerous pathways for deception.

The following five keys can help protect us from the wiles of a counterfeit leader:

1. **Pursue a deeper understanding of Biblical concepts.** There exists a vast difference between *knowing about God* and actually *knowing God*. We can say something similar about the difference between knowing the key doctrines of the Bible and *understanding* their dynamics. Proclaiming truth helps lay a solid foundation for young believers, but teaching them to understand and discern truth will take their spiritual lives to another level.

   If I proclaim something to be true, you will decide whether to take my word for it. But if I present you with an understanding of truth, you begin to realize you are taking God's word for it. You will also be better equipped to understand the nature of theological falsehoods.

2. **Encourage people to ask questions.** Proponents of truth should never fear honest questions—even hard ones. Effective learning takes place only in environments where the freedom

to make inquiry is celebrated. We might not answer every question to a person's satisfaction, but simply allowing the opportunity paves the way for deeper understanding.

3. **Preach and model humility.** False prophets often characterize themselves as humble servants of God, but their self-serving actions speak otherwise. One of the best ways to help people recognize counterfeit humility is to present them with a consistent example of the real thing.

4. **Emphasize the importance of good spiritual fruit—or the lack thereof.** People become susceptible when they value gifts above fruit. This should not be an "either/or" scenario; we need both.

    Bad fruit results from the "I will ascend" mentality pioneered by Lucifer (Isaiah 14:12–14). A highly gifted individual might display an air of profound spirituality but still live according to the flesh, guided by human wisdom—or worse.

5. **Preach and model the importance of relationships within the body of Christ.** I see red flags rising when people claim their organization alone represents the "true way of God." Such a proclamation goes hand in hand with isolationist tendencies. Leaders who exalt their organization as commissioned by God above others will position their people for deception.

    Close and open relationships within a family or church are also vital. I have seen more than one situation in which a person was spared from the wiles of a counterfeit leader because a connection with mature believers opened his or her eyes to the dangers.

I wish I could say we should trust any organization employing the name "Christian" or "church." Unfortunately, counterfeits remain abundant, so teaching people to discern the signs of counterfeit spirituality should be a high priority. We might also need to help some of them work through the deep sense of disillusionment that so often results from being under the influence of a counterfeit leader.

Counterfeit leaders create manipulative, controlling, and unhealthy spiritual environments. Too often, though, noble-sounding words blind people to the dysfunction. For those who finally escape the deception, healing might take a very long time. If such individuals begin attending your church, provide them with the time and opportunity to work through their pain and confusion, regardless of how gifted or experienced in ministry they appear to be.

THE BOTTOM LINE

Counterfeit leaders are an unfortunate and dangerous reality in our world. A necessary part of helping people grow to maturity involves training them to understand truth and to recognize the warning signs of a spiritual fraud.

RELEVANT QUESTIONS

1. Have you had any personal experience with counterfeit leaders?
2. What is significant about Jesus' statements in Matthew 7:15–23?
3. What did the Lord mean when He said, "You will know them by their fruits"?
4. What are some marks of a counterfeit leader?
5. What stands out to you about Paul's comments in Acts 20:28–31 regarding "savage wolves"?
6. What is significant about referring to counterfeit leaders, including false prophets, as wolves?
7. How does growing toward spiritual maturity protect people from the lure of a counterfeit leader?
8. Talk about the dynamics of the following keys:

a. Pursue an understanding of Biblical concepts.
   b. Encourage people to ask questions.
   c. Preach and model humility.
   d. Emphasize the importance of spiritual fruit—or the lack thereof.
   e. Preach and model the importance of relationships within the body of Christ.
9. Can you think of any other steps we can take to help protect our people from counterfeit leaders?
10. What would you recommend for someone who has come out from under the influence of a counterfeit leader?

CHAPTER TWENTY-TWO

CARING FOR OURSELVES

As much as we hate to admit it, human nature is prone to deception and error. That is why we, like sheep, tend to go astray (Isaiah 53:6). We are also likely to misunderstand or distort important concepts, and so nuanced teaching is necessary.

Previously, I presented a negative perspective of self-love while also emphasizing the importance of self-denial. That does not mean, however, that we should neglect our personal needs as a matter of practice.

In Christian environments that encourage wholehearted devotion to God, people often live under a burden of guilt, feeling selfish for taking time off or doing something enjoyable. This type of service carries no joy and easily leads to burnout.

I will be the first to claim that some have abused the concept of self-care by confusing it with self-indulgence. Still, we err badly when we abandon the basic principles of self-care in the name of faithful Christian ministry.

Service to God is like a marathon, not a sprint. And if we fail to care for ourselves properly, we will limit the good we can do for others. We might even become the focus of ministry instead of giving attention to other people in need. Broken health, a failing marriage, and estranged children are *not* necessary byproducts of an effective ministry.

Because our time and resources are limited, saying "yes" to one thing always means saying "no" to another. But saying "no" is almost always more difficult. Our world has more needs than any person, church, or denomination can ever begin to meet. This is our stark reality. If we attempt to satisfy them all, we will drive ourselves into the ground and destroy our families in the process.

Caring and conscientious people forever face the temptation to follow their conscience over the leading of the Holy Spirit. What turmoil we experience when we fall short or feel as though we let someone down! Even when the Holy Spirit leads us away from meeting a particular need, feelings of guilt and regret can linger for a long time.

We can also exhaust ourselves by dwelling in the world of comparison-based living. The Lord created each of us with unique gifts and abilities to accomplish unique purposes. What frustration we create by attempting to duplicate another person's life and ministry! The resulting pressure comes not from God but from a misrepresentation of a true identity.

SERVING FROM OVERFLOW

We cannot give what we do not have, and we cannot do what God has not given us the grace to accomplish. By His design, effective Christian service is always the product of *overflow*.

Effective ministry comes not from our innate ability but from an intimate relationship with the One who created us. When He walked this earth, Jesus profoundly stated, "I can do nothing on My own initiative" (John 5:30).

Everything Jesus said and did was an extension of His relationship with His heavenly Father. And if that was true for God's only begotten Son, how much more do you and I need guidance and empowerment from heaven?

By nature, we are *dependents*. We rely upon air to breathe, water to drink, and food to eat. And spiritually speaking, we are no less so. All we have, all we are, and all we do are the overflows of heaven's grace. And thankfully for us, that overflow does not lack in any way:

> "He who believes in Me, as the Scripture said, 'From his innermost being will flow rivers of living water.'" John 7:38

The secret to serving well lies in receiving well. But pride will always hinder us from drawing upon the wellspring of heaven. From the day our ancestors fell in Eden, humans have sought to see themselves as gods. And even true servants of the Lord are enticed into thinking they can run the race of life without stopping to rest and refuel. Time always proves them wrong, however, and the results are never pretty.

The one who cares for body and soul recognizes the reality of our human limitations. Soul care is not selfish. And what we call "selflessness" can sometimes be a matter of pride. We might portray a noble, selfless image not because we are selfless, but so others can gawk like tourists in awe of our profound devotion.

Why do we practice self-care? The basic principles of rest are rooted in Scripture, and there is nothing spiritually noble about ignoring them. If we truly value our long-term service to God and the meaningful relationships in our lives, we will learn the art of resting.

Working nonstop might seem noble and spiritual, but such a lifestyle flows from prideful disobedience. Even under the old covenant law, God provided—and commanded—rest for His people (Exodus 20:8–11). Today, some of our significant options include:

- **Daily devotions** – If we do not cultivate personal, intimate time with the Lord through worship, prayer, and the reading of the Word, we have only our own strength and wisdom to offer. If you want to burn out, neglect your daily time with

God. But if you want to lead and serve effectively, make it a point to sit daily at the Lord's feet.

- **A day of rest** – It was God who observed the first Sabbath as He modeled a necessary practice for us (Genesis 2:1–3). And Israel observed its first Sabbath even before the Ten Commandments were given (Exodus 16:22–30). For the Christian, the Sabbath is not an obligation but an *invitation* to set aside the labors of life to renew faith and family. It is not noble, but prideful, for Christian leaders to work 24/7.

- **Spiritual retreats** – Taking time away from our responsibilities to read, pray, and seek the Lord can provide a powerful means to renew our relationship with God and our ability to serve Him effectively.

- **Personal time to disconnect** – The weights of life and ministry can drive us into the ground. To avoid negative long-term consequences, we need to disconnect from our responsibilities routinely. One viable option is to find a hobby that will help you break free and renew your focus. Just be sure that the hobby serves you and not vice versa.

- **Vacations** – Of course, we want to stay within our financial means, but vacations can provide an excellent opportunity to cultivate relationships and renew the soul. Also, parents from all walks of life can use vacations to build and maintain family relationships in a way that complements their day-to-day efforts.

One of the great dangers of working 24/7 is that we become the "gods" of our work. We own it; it belongs to us. But the Lord only gives grace for us to do *His* work. Taking time off compels us to let go of control and restore ownership to the Creator of all things. Then, as we let go and disconnect, the Holy Spirit provides the grace for us to labor effectively. But if we do not surrender ownership back to God, the full weight of responsibility becomes ours.

I would also argue that the need for rest is greater than ever because of our technological era. Early on, technology promised an easier lifestyle. Today, we know better. Thanks to human invention, we now have instant access to work demands, more exposure to the concerns of our era, and more decisions to process.

Young people, in particular, often struggle because they have never known a life apart from computers, cell phones, and social media. Soul care, it seems, is becoming more of a necessity than a luxury.

Leaders not only learn and teach, they also model. And you can be sure that those who follow are watching. Not only do our work habits affect us and our families, they also influence those involved with our organizations. If we preach about the need for rest but refuse to apply the principles ourselves, our people will feel pressured to labor nonstop. Devoted congregants then become guilt-ridden, frazzled, and burned-out. Their resulting hesitancy to serve will in turn create frustrated pastors, perpetuating a vicious cycle.

So while we should model the importance of devotion and hard work, we also want to provide an example that allows our people to rest and care for themselves and their families. In this, we walk a fine line between aggressively seeking to advance God's kingdom while also accommodating the realistic needs of everyone involved.

THE BOTTOM LINE

As we teach about the importance of love and self-denial, let us also remember that effective ministry is the product of overflow. By teaching and modeling soul care, we can empower our people to serve the Lord effectively over the long term.

RELEVANT QUESTIONS

1. What is the difference between self-care and self-love?
2. Why are devoted Christians tempted to believe that spiritual people must work nonstop?
3. How does the inability to say "no" factor into serving God effectively?
4. What are your criteria for saying "yes" or "no"?
5. When it comes to meeting needs, how can we distinguish between the leading of the Holy Spirit and the sense of obligation that our conscience might press upon us?
6. How does our tendency to compare ourselves with others factor into the pressure to work nonstop?
7. What are some consequences of neglecting healthy soul care?
8. Talk about any experiences you have had with burnout.
9. What does John 7:38 speak to you?
10. Why must ministry always be a matter of overflow?
11. Why is it prideful to neglect healthy self-care?
12. Talk about how you incorporate the following into your life:
    a. Daily devotions
    b. A weekly Sabbath
    c. Personal retreats or sabbaticals
    d. Time to disconnect and surrender control back to God
    e. Vacations
13. Why does modern technology make rest more of a need than a luxury?
14. Provide some practical steps that people can take to make technology serve them instead of them serving technology.

CHAPTER TWENTY-THREE

GLORIFYING GOD

I have had significant questions about worship at different times during my life. Before I became a Christian, the idea of worshipping Jesus made little sense. "I would be deeply thankful if a friend sacrificed his life by jumping on a hand grenade for me," I once said, "but I wouldn't worship him. So, while I'm very appreciative of Christ's sacrifice on the cross for my sins, I don't see a need to worship Him either."

Through the process of becoming a Christian, my eyes were opened. I came to recognize the divinity of Jesus, which destroyed my previous reasoning. Still, for a very long time, I struggled with the idea of God wanting to receive worship. The best comparison I could make was with a dastardly villain in a superhero movie who wanted everyone to bow at his feet—or die! The idea of a benevolent God who received worship did not seem to fit.

I do not think I am the only person to ask questions about worship, so I see value in exploring the issue. But where do we begin?

THE CHARACTER OF GOD

To compare the holy and majestic Creator of our universe with a sinister villain is to put God on the same level as the devil. Few theological errors are as bad! We know the evil one's end goal through his temptation of Jesus in the wilderness:

> Again, the devil took Him to a very high mountain and showed Him all the kingdoms of the world and their glory; and he said to Him, "All these things I will give You, if You fall down and worship me." Matthew 4:8–9

The devil and his demons *crave* glory and will seek it by any means possible. God, on the other hand, is the *source* of all glory. He craves *nothing* in that regard. Because the desire for glory permeates the core of our beings, we struggle to grasp His perspective. Human glory is a cheap and fleeting substitute for the real thing, but that does not stop us from seeking our fill.

To gain a better understanding of these issues, we must consider the character of Jesus Christ, who walked this earth as God in human flesh. What we see in Jesus through the Scriptures, we see by faith in the heavenly Father (John 14:1–11).

From before the beginning of time, Jesus stood at the pinnacle of heavenly glory. But for our benefit, the Son of God laid aside His lofty status to take human form—with all its natural functions and limitations. But Jesus went lower still by embracing the shame of crucifixion on a Roman cross.

Jesus Christ went from the highest to the lowest, and because of this, God the Father exalted Him to the highest place once again (Philippians 2:5–11). By His actions, the Son of God proved Himself worthy of all glory and honor and power. He also showed He could handle being worshipped without His ego being inflated.

Psalm 22:3 tells us that God *inhabits* the praises of His people. When we praise and worship the Lord, we align with a universal reality: our Creator is worthy of all glory and honor and power.

On the day that we call "Palm Sunday," Jesus descended from the Mount of Olives on a donkey (Luke 19:28–40). As Christ's followers began to praise and worship, the Pharisees recoiled in horror. "Teacher, rebuke Your disciples," they admonished. The Lord's response was one for the ages: "I tell you, if these become silent, the stones will cry out!" *Worship has nothing to do with feeding God's ego; it is about aligning with the reality of creation.*

All creation bursts with glory, pointing to God as its source. If the Lord were to deny His worthiness, He would be a liar. And so God receives worship, but not in an egotistical way.

We could take this argument a step further by considering the New Testament references to glory. A pattern emerges in that the Father, Son, and Holy Spirit seek to glorify *one another*. I do not entirely understand it, but I know enough to see the selfless love of God at work.

NO OTHER GODS BEFORE ME

The very first of the Ten Commandments proclaims, "You shall have no other gods before Me" (Exodus 20:3). And while this statement might *appear* egotistical, we must consider the context. The people of Israel dwelt in an idolatrous environment. We know this both from the Bible and archaeology. Most cultures worshipped multiple gods, and even as Moses handed down the First Commandment, the people of Israel became ensnared by worshipping a golden calf.

"What is the problem with worshipping idols?" you might ask. Behind every idol—whether it be of wood, silver, or gold—a demon spirit seeks glorification (1 Corinthians 10:19–20). At its core, idolatry is demonic. We see some of the rotten fruit through the sexual immorality, human sacrifice, and other forms of violence that often accompanied the idol worship of the ancients.

Why does God decry the worship of idols? The spirits behind them are bent on destroying human lives. When we worship God, He releases blessings. But when we worship idols, demons wreak destruction. Of course, it would make sense for the Lord to forbid the worship of false gods. Even in worship, the Lord has our well-being in mind.

Does God expect to receive our worship? Absolutely. But even in this, He is unselfish. Glory, in many ways, is the *elixir of life*. In it, we find the joy, vitality, and significance for which we all long. And when we worship the Lord, He graciously allows us to share the euphoria of the experience. This would not be the approach of an egotist who pursues glory even at the expense of others. The Lord will not share the blessings of His glory with an evil demon, but He does want to share them with the children He so dearly loves (John 17:22).

BIBLE OR CULTURE?

The manner in which we worship God has been a subject of controversy throughout the centuries. How ironic! At the core of worship is a heartfelt love for God, yet we do not seem to hesitate to criticize His beloved children whose styles of worship differ from ours.

To worship God is Biblical, but our modes and methods involve more of a cultural dynamic. During King David's time, the people of God worshipped with a variety of musical instruments. But the New Testament is silent in this regard. Many early Christians avoided using musical instruments in worship because they wanted to maintain a clean break from Judaism, among other reasons.

Later, because of its secular—and pagan—origins, the *pipe organ* generated considerable controversy when first introduced into church worship. The *piano* received a similar response because it was widely used in saloons and other undesirable places. Today, some Christians criticize worship bands and their variety of instruments—especially drums—thinking the organ to be more sacred. Go figure. Sometimes, I think we become so adept at drawing lines that we paint ourselves into a corner, leaving little room for anyone to move.

Regarding musical styles, some are better suited than others for worship, but again, the state of the heart is what matters most. Modes, methods, and styles change over time, but hearts of worship endure.

A pastor friend of mine once asked an older church member about his opinion regarding the church's contemporary worship. "I don't much like it," the gray-haired senior replied, "but my grandson loves it, and that's good enough for me."

I love that older man's response! In the end, worship is about God and His purposes, not us. Sure, we all have our preferences, but it is unwise to allow them to taint our theology. What matters most is that God is glorified and younger generations are drawn.

We can say something similar regarding *musical styles*. Many old hymns brim with rich theology, and almost as importantly, they can be sung easily by "musical morons" like me who cannot carry a tune across the street. While many contemporary songs touch hearts with the truths of Scripture, they can also be difficult for the untrained to follow. And so it is that a worship service can quickly become a performance in which the congregation stands closed mouthed, watching the musicians express their passions. I think wisdom encourages us to make room for both the old and new.

WORSHIP AS MOTIVATION

Why is it that we argue about modes and methods of worship? Praising and worshipping God provides an amazing opportunity not only to exalt the Lord, but also to enter His presence. Individual preferences matter little; His worthiness matters most.

Worship is our *response* to who God is and what He has done for us. Song, declaration, and silence are all acceptable, but worship does not stop there. Just about all we do should be an extension of our worship. This means that the line between sacred and secular work is thin, if a line exists at all. *Just about anything done to glorify God can be considered sacred, and the motives behind our actions generally determine whether our works are living or dead.*

Two people can take the same actions, while driven by profoundly different motives. Dead works find their roots in a self-focus. Self-preservation, self-fulfillment, self-validation, and self-glorification can all apply here. But pure worship transcends self, and it cannot help but go beyond our words. A heart intent on glorifying God will seek to honor the Lord through attitude and word, with actions surely in tow.

A wise leader does not seek to motivate people by inflicting feelings of obligation and guilt. Such efforts will keep believers mired in immaturity. They can also lead to burnout. A truly wise leader helps to cultivate a sincere love for God expressed through uncorrupted worship.

Do you want to motivate your people? Help them fall in love with Jesus. "We love, because He first loved us" (1 John 4:19). It really is that simple. As we spotlight God's goodness and glory, and as people grasp the contrast between the depths of sin and their lofty status in Christ, love and gratitude cannot help but fill their hearts.

Show me a person who truly sees Jesus, and I will show you someone who lives for God. Perhaps Peter and John said it best: "We cannot stop speaking about what we have seen and heard" (Acts 4:20). And like Peter and John, they will view personal sacrifice for the Lord as pure honor. A grateful desire to glorify God will always move people further than a sense of duty or obligation ever could.

THE BOTTOM LINE

God alone is worthy of the highest glory, and God alone can receive that glory without becoming self-absorbed. When we worship the Lord with music and song, we align with a universal reality, which brings us near to His presence. And while the heart of worship is always more important than the mode or method, a truly worshipful heart will also find expression in our attitudes and actions.

RELEVANT QUESTIONS

1. Please read Revelation 22:8–9. How did the angel respond when John fell at his feet in worship?
2. Please read John 20:24–29. What is significant about Jesus' response when Thomas called Him, "My Lord and my God"?
3. How is human glory a cheap imitation of the real thing?
4. Why is God alone worthy of glory?
5. How do we know God is not egotistical about receiving worship?
6. Why might we call glory "the elixir of our spiritual lives"?
7. Please read Psalm 22:3. What does it mean that God inhabits the praises of His people?
8. How does the worship of idols affect our lives?
9. How are we affected when we worship God?
10. Why is the heart of worship more important than the mode or method of our worship?
11. What determines whether our work is sacred or secular?
12. Why is love a more powerful motivator than duty or obligation?

CHAPTER TWENTY-FOUR

CULTIVATING FAITHFULNESS

We all have shortcomings and issues; they are part of being human. Where we end in life, however, should differ greatly from where we begin, and one quality stands as important as any other when it comes to spiritual growth: *faithfulness*.

Culture views faithfulness as a virtue, but few seem to adopt it as a lifestyle. Faithfulness begins with God. He is *absolutely* faithful to His promises and has never failed to uphold even one. Circumstances, however, can often send a different message.

Psalm 89 provides a perfect example of our human struggle to understand God's faithfulness. The Psalmist begins by recounting the Lord's promises to King David and his descendants, remembering His faithfulness to covenant relationships:

> "But I will not break off My lovingkindness from him,
> Nor deal falsely in My faithfulness.
> My covenant I will not violate,
> Nor will I alter the utterance of My lips.
> Once I have sworn by My holiness;
> I will not lie to David.
> His descendants shall endure forever
> And his throne as the sun before Me.
> It shall be established forever like the moon,
> And the witness in the sky is faithful." Selah.
> Psalm 89:33–37

The unwavering consistency of daily sunrises and sunsets provides a practical reminder of the Lord's faithfulness, and the Psalmist knew it well. But then Psalm 89 takes a troubling turn:

> But You have cast off and rejected,
> You have been full of wrath against Your anointed.
> You have spurned the covenant of Your servant;
> You have profaned his crown in the dust.
> You have broken down all his walls;
> You have brought his strongholds to ruin.
> All who pass along the way plunder him;
> He has become a reproach to his neighbors.
> You have exalted the right hand of his adversaries;
> You have made all his enemies rejoice.
> You also turn back the edge of his sword
> And have not made him stand in battle.
> You have made his splendor to cease
> And cast his throne to the ground.
> Psalm 89:38–44

"How," wondered the Psalmist, "can our faithful God allow us to experience such devastating humiliation?" And it was not just the random, seemingly senseless type of suffering that God's people so often question. The Lord appeared to abandon a clear and firm *promise* He had made to King David.

We are blessed to view this passage from a perspective the people of ancient Israel could not. How could they possibly envision the Son of God coming to earth as the Son of Man, dying for the sins of the people, and resurrecting from the grave to rule as David's heir for all eternity? Even though visible circumstances pointed toward broken promises, the Lord was faithful through it all, without fail. In this, Psalm 89 provides a powerful lesson for all who seek to walk with God.

The absolute faithfulness of God is the stability of our times, no matter what our times happen to be.

FAITHFULNESS IS FOUNDATIONAL

The line between faithfulness, trustworthiness, and faith is thin—if such a line exists at all. Faithfulness begets faith, and faith begets faithfulness. Those who recognize our Creator's faithfulness to His unwavering promises will become steadfast and faithful themselves—even in the face of adversity.

Being faithful means being true to our word even when it hurts. And it means consistently following through on the things God calls us to do regardless of the cost. Being unfaithful undermines trust, making genuine intimacy elusive. It also hamstrings our ability to accomplish plans and projects. Forward progress is bound to stall without faithful participation.

Throughout my years of ministry, I have found faithfulness to be an essential foundation for growth and transformation. When I served as a campus minister, I could usually predict a student's growth based on his or her consistency in attending Bible study meetings. Those who attended faithfully would grow, and those who did not would often miss the lessons they needed most. Not all who were faithful grew toward maturity, but I cannot recall meaningful growth among the inconsistent.

Christians sometimes err by failing to discern what God expects of them. More often than not, people react to the need of the moment, rather than seeking a clear vision for what He wants them to do. They spread their focus in too many directions, and thus fail to do anything well. *We do not need to do everything; we just need to be faithful to what we commit to in obedience to God.*

WHY BE FAITHFUL?

Christians often spread themselves too thin because they do not want to appear as unloving, but the roots of godly faithfulness also stem from a loving heart. Why do we follow through with our promises? We value and care about people. Why do we serve with faithfulness and integrity? We value and care about people.

Why do we conduct business in an honest and trustworthy manner? Once again, we value and care about people.

While others might not always recognize and applaud faithfulness, you can be sure that unfaithfulness will be forever remembered. Whether it involves violating marriage vows, breaking promises to a child, or presenting a poor witness of Christ, the fruit of unfaithfulness seems to sprout like weeds.

Deciding to plant a garden, I once ordered a truckload of topsoil from an advertisement in the classified ads. When the man showed up at my home, I immediately noticed Bible verses displayed across the sides of his truck. Explaining that he had a full load, he asked if I would be willing to purchase all the dirt instead of just the half load I had ordered. I agreed to help out someone I thought was a brother in Christ. But when he dumped the topsoil, it was filled with large clumps of clay. I came away disappointed and could not help but wonder what kind of witness his actions would have presented to a nonbeliever. How these negative experiences stick with us! Even after forty years, with no effort I can still recall that man's lack of integrity!

None of us can identify as God, and so circumstances beyond our control will sometimes derail our good intentions. Still, we do our best to live with integrity, and that means following through when we make plans with someone. We should also make promises sparingly, doing so only when confident that we can keep them.

In the times we fall short, we should humble ourselves, apologize, and shake off any condemnation that might try to settle into our hearts. The primary issue, however, is not whether we sometimes fail to keep a promise, but what *characterizes* us. If we are characteristically faithful, most people will give grace for an occasional failure to follow through.

Ultimately, we live faithfully because we want to honor the God we profess to serve. Our faithfulness reflects His glory. And of this you can be sure, He will always remember our faithful service—even when others do not.

> For God is not unjust so as to forget your work and the love which you have shown toward His name, in having ministered and in still ministering to the saints.
> Hebrews 6:10

Most of us long to hear the affirming words Jesus extended to the wise servant in the Parable of the Talents: "Well done, good and faithful servant" (Matthew 25:23, ESV). The Lord will not speak these words indiscriminately, but only to those who did indeed live faithfully on earth. Those who are faithful in obscurity, the Lord will one day honor in full view among a vast multitude!

THE BOTTOM LINE

There are not many absolutes in this world, but God is absolutely faithful to His Word. If we truly believe this, we will become faithful ourselves. Such steadfast character through times good and bad will create a stronghold of stability and draw others toward God's goodness. But regardless of how others respond, the Lord will always remember and bless the faithfulness of His beloved servants.

RELEVANT QUESTIONS

1. Why is God absolutely faithful to His promises?
2. Why is faithfulness becoming a lost quality in our day?
3. How has our drift from covenantal thinking affected our perspective of faithfulness?
4. Why is it a mistake to judge God's faithfulness based on our circumstances?
5. How is faithfulness rooted in faith?
6. How is faithfulness also rooted in love?
7. Why do you think people tend to remember unfaithful words and actions?

8. Why are we often tempted to do more than we can effectively manage?
9. What does it mean to be faithful to one's word?
10. What does it mean to be faithful to a spouse?
11. What does it mean to be faithful to the Lord?
12. What comfort and encouragement can we find in knowing that God remembers all the unseen things we do from hearts of faithful love?

Section Five

Making a Difference

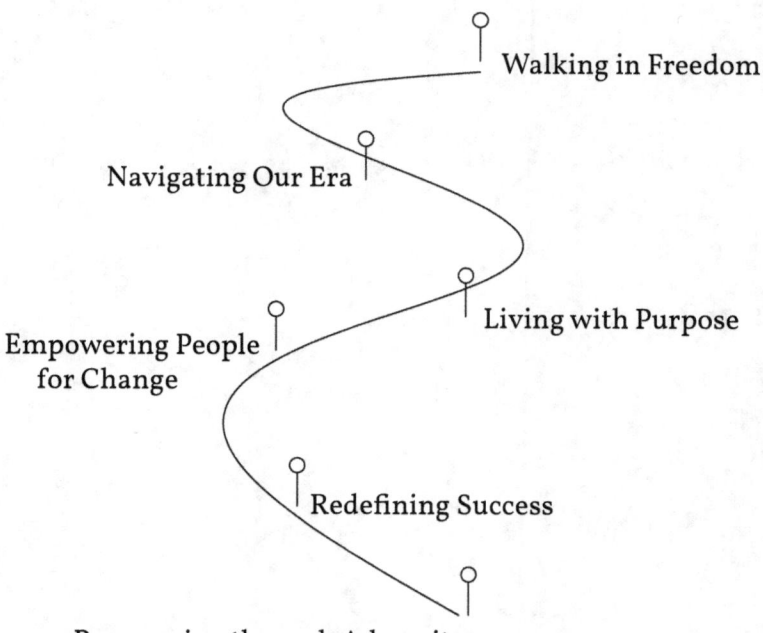

My Father is glorified by this, that you bear much fruit, and so prove to be My disciples. Just as the Father has loved Me, I have also loved you; abide in My love.

John 15:8–9

CHAPTER TWENTY-FIVE

WALKING IN FREEDOM

Not long ago, Debi and I visited Monticello—the home of Thomas Jefferson—for a tour. What an interesting experience that was! I had heard bits and pieces about this founding father of the United States, but a closer look helped me better understand Jefferson's core motivations.

Despite serving two terms as the third President of the United States of America, along with having filled several other high-ranking government positions, Jefferson requested that only the following be engraved on his tombstone: "HERE WAS BURIED THOMAS JEFFERSON AUTHOR OF THE DECLARATION OF AMERICAN INDEPENDENCE OF THE STATUTE OF VIRGINIA FOR RELIGIOUS FREEDOM & FATHER OF THE UNIVERSITY OF VIRGINIA."

All three of the items identified by Jefferson found their roots in a basic underlying principle that characterized his perspective on life: the need for *self-governance.*

Jefferson and his contemporaries were well aware of the political dynamics of Europe, along with the use of public religion to manipulate and control the masses. In Thomas Jefferson's mind, personal freedom of religion and universal education both served the purpose of self-governance. Each individual was free to live by his own conscience toward God—a mindset informed by religion, morality, and knowledge of humanity.

Jefferson felt that religion helped form the basis of morality. And he especially esteemed the teachings and morals of Jesus, while also denying any miraculous workings in or through Christ.

Jefferson's ideas and efforts touched on a universal desire for *freedom*. A mysterious drive deep within the human heart yearns to be free. Freedom for the common person, however, has proven elusive throughout history. For years, the foundation of freedom laid by Jefferson and his contemporaries in the US Constitution has stood as a landmark of hope for our world. But times have changed, and we are seeing the precarious nature of true freedom. In all this, I cannot help but wonder about God's perspective on the issue.

ESTABLISHING A BIBLICAL PERSPECTIVE

When considering the Bible, I would venture the average person thinks "restrictions" rather than "freedom." Ironically, the first allusion to freedom in the Bible also identifies the first restriction. The setting was the garden of Eden:

> The Lord God commanded the man, saying, "From any tree of the garden you may eat freely; but from the tree of the knowledge of good and evil you shall not eat, for in the day that you eat from it you will surely die." Genesis 2:16–17

This simple statement overflows with theological meaning. To begin, God gave humanity the freedom to eat from an almost unlimited menu of choices. We have no way of knowing how many species of vegetables, berries, and fruit grew in Eden, but if it is even close to today, Adam and Eve likely had *hundreds*, if not *thousands*, of choices.

Our Creator also gave the first human parents *one* lone restriction: they could not eat from the tree of the knowledge of good and evil without suffering severe consequences. Thousands of choices with only one restriction? That sounds pretty free to me. But why would God make any restrictions at all?

THE TWO TREES

It speaks volumes that God put both the tree of life *and* the tree of the knowledge of good and evil in the garden of Eden. Genesis 2:9 tells us He placed the tree of life in the middle of the garden. The tree of the knowledge of good and evil, it seems, was not far off. The proximity of these trees highlights the element of *choice* the Lord gave to humanity from the very beginning.

Genesis 1:26-28 tells us that God created humans "in His image." Exactly what this means is difficult to establish, but we can identify several significant elements. For example, our authority to rule over the earth (also given in Genesis 1:26-28) reflects His reign as King over all creation.

Also vital to our context is the Biblical statement that "God is love" (1 John 4:8). The unconditional love of God points toward His freeness because true love requires freedom.

Cultures all over our globe celebrate the virtues of love, but what makes it so special? Freedom! It exhilarates us when someone whom we see as significant chooses, without compulsion, to see us as special. But without freedom, love loses its luster. If I somehow programmed my wife to love me, it would not be love.

By giving Adam and Eve the freedom to choose between the two trees, our Creator gave humanity the opportunity to love just like Him. But the freedom to love also requires the freedom to "not love," which opens the door for depths of pain that are hardly imaginable.

And so, from the very beginning, our Creator provided humanity with a measure of freedom. That freedom can never be absolute, however, because we are finite creatures who need boundaries for our well-being. Think about the road signs, painted lines, and guardrails along a busy highway. Without them, deadly accidents would abound. Similarly, if God were to remove all the boundaries He has established for us, we would not last long.

Even with boundaries in place, we have the freedom to transgress them at our peril. Love and freedom mutually depend upon one another. Just as love cannot exist without freedom, so freedom cannot prosper without love. The freedom championed by Thomas Jefferson, for example, could only last if people governed themselves by choosing to limit their selfish tendencies to benefit the common good. As much as we might want to think otherwise, selfish actions have far-reaching implications.

GOD'S SOVEREIGNTY VERSUS OUR FREE WILL

One of the great controversies of the church stems from the relationship between *God's sovereignty* and our *human free will*. This need not be a source of argument, but opposing camps argue nonetheless, citing a variety of Bible verses to support their positions. The truth is that both can and do exist at once, although we lack the ability to draw a clear line between them.

In essence, God is sovereign and rules over all that exists. No one has the power to question His supreme authority, nothing can hinder Him from doing what He wants, and He depends upon nothing for His existence. At the same time, our God has chosen to give us the freedom to make personal choices for which we are accountable. Our choices also have consequences, which we cannot control.

Mysteriously, our Creator can take our free choices and work them toward His sovereign purposes. How He does that, we do not know. I suppose it is part of what makes Him "God."

Regarding sovereignty and free will, we will always feel a tension. And that is okay. The bigger problem results when we focus on one to the exclusion of the other. Blurring and distortion result—similar to what we see in the world of photography.

If I adjust a camera's optics to snap a picture of a wedding couple, for example, I can capture bride and groom in exquisite detail. But in doing so, the background becomes blurred. And if I focus on background detail, my view of the couple then blurs. Nothing changes about the couple or the background; the only difference involves our limited ability to capture their images.

INTERNAL AND EXTERNAL FREEDOM

Our human freedom exists on two primary levels. The first involves an *external* liberty on which we naturally focus. These "civil liberties" involve the freedom to make individual choices and live free from discrimination regarding issues of speech, religion, etc. Sadly, humans have a long and sordid history of seeking to exert control over other humans. Perhaps the worst violation of a person's civil liberty would involve slavery, which, unfortunately, still exists in many parts of our globe.

A second expression of freedom involves the ability to live in dominion over one's *internal* passions and desires. It is this type of freedom the Bible emphasizes because of its spiritual—and eternal—ramifications.

During the fifteen centuries in which the Bible was penned, powerful people routinely enslaved others for personal gain. Even Abraham's descendants were unjustly oppressed as slaves in Egypt for several hundred years. The Bible used this experience to illuminate important spiritual truths, but never was slavery as an institution condemned—not even in the New Testament. Some people struggle with that thought.

Well aware of Isaiah's prophecy about liberty (Isaiah 61:1), the Jews waited expectantly for a Messiah who would free their people from Roman oppression, but Jesus had a very different kind of freedom in mind:

> So Jesus was saying to those Jews who had believed Him, "If you continue in My word, then you are truly

> disciples of Mine; and you will know the truth, and the truth will make you free." They answered Him, "We are Abraham's descendants and have never yet been enslaved to anyone; how is it that You say, 'You will become free'?"
>
> Jesus answered them, "Truly, truly, I say to you, everyone who commits sin is the slave of sin. The slave does not remain in the house forever; the son does remain forever. So if the Son makes you free, you will be free indeed." John 8:31–36

Christ's statement is both theological and hopeful. Any promise of freedom cheers the heart, but the path to real and lasting liberty does not require violence or weapons of war. Instead, it results from an intimate understanding and embrace of God's reality.

When the New Testament addresses the topic of freedom, it focuses primarily on *spiritual freedom from sin*. How alien these perspectives of suffering and freedom are to humanity! Rare is the person who values spiritual freedom to such a high degree.

In the midst of unimaginable difficulty, the Lord can bring eternal blessings. And so it was that Christ's apostles *rejoiced* at the honor of suffering for the Lord (Acts 5:41). They knew their suffering was not in vain and that the Lord would one day reward them beyond measure.

During His time of ministry on our planet, Jesus focused on issues of the heart rather than trying to change human institutions. After His departure from earth, His disciples did the same. Only later did Christ's followers confront the institution of slavery in various nations.

Why did God focus on the heart rather than the institution? We cannot say with complete clarity, but He seems to embrace a pattern of transforming human hearts that will then transform human institutions.

We should never think lightly about slavery and similar forms of oppression on our planet. But even those in the most dire circumstances can find great hope through the Scriptures!

FREEDOM FROM SIN'S DOMINION

When Adam and Eve disobeyed God and ate from the tree of the knowledge of good and evil, they made a free choice; there was nothing to compel them. That foolish choice, however, opened the door for sin to dominate and control all humanity. And sin does not a nice slave owner make; its power is cruel, oppressive, and destructive. The picture of Israel's bondage under Pharaoh in Egypt helps us understand this unfortunate truth (Exodus 1).

Sin gains its power as we are indebted to moral and religious perfection under law-based standards. According to the insightful apostle Paul:

> "Therefore let it be known to you, brethren, that through Him forgiveness of sins is proclaimed to you, and through Him everyone who believes is freed from all things, from which you could not be freed through the Law of Moses." Acts 13:38–39

What amazing and wonderful news! Few things in this world breed hopelessness like being bound by sin, and few are as exhilarating as being freed from that bondage.

Freedom, however, is not unlimited, which is illustrated by a progression of thought found in Paul's letter to the Galatians:

> It was for freedom that Christ set us free; therefore keep standing firm and do not be subject again to a yoke of slavery. Galatians 5:1

> For you were called to freedom, brethren; only do not turn your freedom into an opportunity for the flesh, but through love serve one another. Galatians 5:13

> But I say, walk by the Spirit, and you will not carry out the desire of the flesh. For the flesh sets its desire against the Spirit, and the Spirit against the flesh; for these are in opposition to one another, so that you may not do the things that you please. Galatians 5:16–17

VOLUNTARY BOND-SERVANTS

Once again, an Old Testament example can help us better grasp a New Testament reality. The law of Moses gave ancient Jews the right to buy and sell slaves, but not permanently (Exodus 21:1–6). Every seven years, these slaves could go free without payment.

However, if a slave had a kind and loving master, and if he felt his conditions were favorable, he could choose to remain with the master permanently. A secure life under an amazing master made the loss of freedom worthwhile. And we can only imagine that such a master would reward this choice with a significant measure of freedom.

Christ has set us free from bondage to the law of sin and death, but because God is such a great and loving Master who watches over us and cares for our needs, we can choose to become His "bond-servants." Motivated by love, Paul adopted just such a mindset (Romans 1:1).

Paul's bond-servant mentality involved two primary dynamics. First, Paul voluntarily restricted his behavior for the benefit of others (Romans 14:13–22). Yes, the gospel of grace brought him an amazing measure of freedom, but the apostle's deep-rooted love compelled him to put the well-being of others above his own desires.

Paul's mindset reflects the heart of a healthy marriage. A man so loves a woman that he freely enters into the marriage covenant, choosing to deny any fleshly desires that would lead to sexual interaction with another person. In his lovestruck eyes, the benefit gained far exceeds anything lost by voluntary restrictions.

WALKING IN FREEDOM

The second bond-servant dynamic involves the motivation to give and serve. Genuine love carries a passion that seeks to bless others. And in Paul's case, his love for God compelled him to go to great lengths to bring the gospel to the unsaved.

The Christian life is to be characterized by *good works*. We are not talking about doing good works in a futile attempt to gain God's favor. Rather, our love and appreciation for His goodness compel us to make a difference in human lives. Exactly what that means will differ for everyone, but the underlying drive to give and serve remains universal for all who have experienced freedom through the cross of Christ.

THE BOTTOM LINE

Freedom is integral to Christian living. But the type of freedom celebrated in the New Testament differs from the self-centered behavior that modern culture defines as freedom. In God's kingdom, love is always the primary means of self-governance.

Freedom and love cannot be separated. Love requires freedom, or it ceases to be love. And freedom can never last without love being its primary motivation. Genuine love constrains our actions and compels us to give and serve for the glory of God.

RELEVANT QUESTIONS

1. When you think of the Bible, do you think "freedom" or "restrictions"?
2. What does it mean to be made in God's image, and why is it so special?
3. How many restrictions did God give in the garden of Eden?
4. Why are love and freedom mutually dependent?
5. What are we missing when we argue about the line between God's sovereignty and our human free will?

6. What is the difference between internal and external freedom?
7. Why does the Bible champion internal freedom over external?
8. How does the picture of Israel's slavery in Egypt help us better understand the freedom God provides from sin's dominion?
9. What are the two primary dynamics of voluntary bond-service to God?
10. Why must love always be our primary motivation for good works?

CHAPTER TWENTY-SIX

NAVIGATING OUR ERA

Have you ever watched the news and asked, "What in the world is going on?" Many of the people you serve have been asking that very question. Our world appears to be spinning wildly out of control. Divisiveness, corruption on both the right and left, out-of-control crime, sexual confusion, economic upheaval, blind zeal, and mass violence are just a few of the many issues marking modern life. The chaos we have long watched from afar has now visited the Western world, and we are struggling to adjust.

The apostle Paul, in his final preserved letter, wrote about what we commonly call the "last days":

> But realize this, that in the last days difficult times will come. For men will be lovers of self, lovers of money, boastful, arrogant, revilers, disobedient to parents, ungrateful, unholy, unloving, irreconcilable, malicious gossips, without self-control, brutal, haters of good, treacherous, reckless, conceited, lovers of pleasure rather than lovers of God, holding to a form of godliness, although they have denied its power; Avoid such men as these. 2 Timothy 3:1–5

It is natural to question where we are regarding Christ's return. And while we see Paul's prophetic insight being fulfilled in our world, it is difficult to establish an exact timeline for these last days. Even Jesus, after addressing the signs of the times, admonished His followers that He did not know the exact timing of His return (Matthew 24:36). That, of course, has not stopped people from proclaiming the specific day of His return. These "seers" have come and gone, and the end has not yet come.

END-TIMES PROPHECY

People often fixate on end-times prophecy, but the fruit of those efforts has not been great. One fundamental problem is that prophecy tends to be cryptic and subject to speculation. I am not suggesting that Bible prophecies are wrong or even unimportant. God always speaks truth, but we do not always have the wisdom, knowledge, and ability to discern what He means.

Think, for a minute, about the Old Testament prophecies concerning Jesus' first coming. They all came to pass, but no one looking forward could grasp what God was up to. Even Jesus' disciples struggled with "prophetic blindness" until after His resurrection. The Lord has given us prophecies about the end for a reason, and so we can draw from them. But we must also take care to hold our interpretations loosely.

The problem with a continual prophetic focus is that we end up chasing ideas, while failing to fulfill the Great Commission. Furthermore, a frightening number of Christians seem to think that the Lord will spare them from hardship, and so they preoccupy themselves with His second coming.

That we are nearing the end, I do not question. The continued degradation of human character, along with rapid advances in technology, stand out among the signs of our times. This is without doubt a historic era for the church, which highlights all the more the importance of our response.

THE PARABLE OF THE SOWER

People naturally moan with anguish and confusion at the decay of culture, while pastors and other Christian leaders play a vital role in helping them navigate this unique era in history. In this, I find Jesus' Parable of the Sower to be highly relevant—especially His comments about the seed that fell among the thorns:

> "Others fell among the thorns, and the thorns came up and choked them out." Matthew 13:7

In His explanation of the parable, we find between Matthew 13 and Luke 8, three specific types of "thorns" that choke out the word of God to render people unfruitful:

1. **The deceitfulness of wealth** – Throughout history, preoccupation with money has distracted people from that which matters most. This is especially true during times of economic upheaval. When people are struggling to make ends meet, it can be difficult for them to focus on anything else. But the wealthy can also be distracted by focusing on earnings and possessions instead of the truly vital elements of life.

2. **The pleasures of life** – Comfort and pleasure are two of the most significant motivating factors even for Christians. And while I do not believe the Lord wants us to be destitute and miserable, He has given us a stewardship to fulfill during our time on earth. We are here for a purpose that far transcends our personal pleasures.

3. **The worry of the age** – This type of thorn is no less deceptive than the other two mentioned by Jesus. Many Christians recognize the gravity of greed and hedonism, but struggle with carrying the heavy burden of our era. This is a collective worry that requires a collective effort to break free.

GAINING HEAVEN'S PERSPECTIVE

Worry and anxiety abound in our day. We are watching human institutions crumble like nothing seen in our lifetime, and even many of God's people struggle to grasp a sense of security. But simply encouraging people to trust God and stop worrying might not be enough. We can help them move toward peace and hope, however, by helping them gain heaven's perspective on the issues of our day.

To begin, we remind even devoted Christians that *the Lord reigns*. No matter what happens in our world, God *always* reigns. He also cares for our needs and will set all things in order in His time (Psalm 97). In talking about the end times, Jesus made a telling statement:

> "You will be hearing of wars and rumors of wars. See that you are not frightened, for those things must take place, but that is not yet the end." Matthew 24:6

I find great comfort in knowing that certain things "must take place." This line of thinking relates closely to "that is not yet the end."

I once flipped a car by foolishly swerving to miss three deer on the road. Thankfully, I came away uninjured, but the crash marked "the end" of that car. The Greek language of Matthew 24:6 reveals that Jesus had a different kind of end in mind, though. To illustrate, NFL football is hugely popular in the United States and even abroad. Each season "ends" with the annual Super Bowl. All the hard work, all the wins and losses, all the good plays and bad plays, even the injuries, all build to a final outcome.

Regarding the end times, we might not entirely understand the dynamics of current events, but we can rest with the confidence that God is using everything to bring about a desired end. The Lord reigns, and He is actively working to accomplish His eternal plans and purposes. *Behind every death-ridden story we see, another story of life unfolds.*

The devil might be intelligent, but hatred has also blinded his eyes. All of hell whistled in delight at the crucifixion of Christ, but had Satan and his demons foreseen what His sacrifice would accomplish, they would have likely kept their distance. Something similar is unfolding in our day. Beyond the chaos and hate seen all around us, the sovereign King over our vast cosmos is working out a divine plan.

In the news, we hear about oppressive governments, international conflicts, and terrorist attacks. But media outlets remain silent regarding the large numbers of people coming to Christ in some of the most oppressed areas of the world. When the Lord moves powerfully through dreams, visions, healings, and miraculous provision, most media outlets turn a blind eye. But that does not stop the Lord from working!

Chaos and upheaval naturally cause brokenness, but broken ground is also necessary for a future harvest. In alignment with the prayers of His people, the Lord is preparing an abundant end-times harvest. How important it is that we be about our Father's business rather than stewing in fret and worry!

Also, we cannot forget that our God is preparing His bride for that great wedding day. Yes, we can be disheartened to see prominent Christian leaders fall into sin and decay, but we can also take comfort in knowing that God is "cleaning house" as He prepares His bride for eternity. The preparation of Christ's bride is no small issue in the eyes of heaven. *Jesus' second coming will not be marked by how bad the world gets as much as by how mature the church becomes.*

Behind every visible story, God's story unfolds. May He grant us grace to move beyond the worry of our age so we can help fulfill His end-times purposes!

THE BOTTOM LINE

Once again, we recognize the importance of faith, love, and wisdom. Through faith, we overcome the anxiety and worry of our age. Through love, we find motivation to make a difference by laboring to advance His kingdom on earth. And, of course, we always need divine wisdom to gain heaven's perspective as we navigate the often-treacherous waters of these last days.

Thankfully, our world is not spinning wildly out of control. As always, God is at work, and we share the privilege of co-laboring for the cause of the gospel.

RELEVANT QUESTIONS

1. What signs of our times tell us that the return of Christ draws ever nearer?
2. Why is it impossible for us to determine the exact date of Jesus' return?
3. What are some dangers of being preoccupied with end-times prophecy?
4. Why is it foolish to think God will spare His people from hardship during these last days?
5. How do the three types of "thorns" choke out God's Word to make human lives unfruitful?
    a. The deceitfulness of wealth
    b. The pleasures of life
    c. The worry of the age
6. How does gaining heaven's perspective of current events help bolster our faith?
7. How do chaos and brokenness help "prepare the ground" for a future harvest of souls?
8. What are some ways in which you see Jesus preparing His bride (the church) for His return?
9. Why are the following essential in our era?
    a. Faith
    b. Love
    c. Wisdom

CHAPTER TWENTY-SEVEN

LIVING WITH PURPOSE

Spiritual maturity involves more than growing in wisdom and refining character. Immature people are consumers; their appetites form the bulk of their decisions. The mature, in contrast, are motivated by purposes beyond themselves.

We should never, however, limit purpose to merely an individual pursuit. All God-given purpose stems from the advancement of His kingdom on earth. And this is the realm in which the Lord intends the *church*—Christ's body—to function. The church has many expressions of love and service, but all should connect to advancing God's kingdom by reaching and helping to grow fully devoted disciples of Christ.

LEADERSHIP PURPOSES

Contrary to popular belief in some circles, the purpose of the church is not to advance the pastor's vision. Too often, we assume that God's vision and the pastor's vision are one and the same, but that is not always the case. I have had times in my life when I sought to fulfill a personal agenda under the guise of advancing God's purposes, and I know I am not alone in this.

Too many times, I have watched pastors use people—in a worldly way—to fulfill their personal agendas. It can be like watching a toddler try to force shapes into the wrong holes on a board, forcing them to fill needs they are unsuited to meet.

People then become expendable resources, and other than a few momentary sighs of disappointment, not much attention is paid when they fall along the wayside. This approach to ministry might bring about numerical growth, but precious lives are damaged, and the weak foundation sets the stage for a future collapse.

One of the keys to effective leadership involves bringing out what God has put within His children. Rather than view people as resources to fulfill *my vision*, I have found purpose in helping others reach *their potential* in Christ. This involves a process of discovery and growth as they learn to draw upon God's grace. Those used by the Lord must endure adversity, but they will always be better for it in the end.

Certain tasks still need to be accomplished, of course. Babies' diapers do not change themselves just because God has called someone to a recovery ministry. But the Lord knows these things. If the body belongs to Him, He will orchestrate people and circumstances to meet the needs. But if we clutch the church tightly as though it were our instrument to fulfill our purposes, it will fall upon us to fill every need.

DISCOVERY OF PURPOSE

A leader's stewardship involves helping people find their place in the body of Christ. When it comes to ministry, God often calls us to tasks that stretch us beyond our natural abilities. In the process, He also forms us for the work He calls us to.

With Christian service, few things are worse than a poor fit. I have known people—pastors included—who were ill-fitted for the work they were trying to accomplish. Driven by human expectations, these well-intentioned souls bred frustration for themselves and the people they served. My own failures in this regard have left a lasting mark. Needless to say, junior high youth ministry holds no place in my future.

Several tools have been designed to help people discover their God-given purposes, and I do not discount their use. For my part, though, I often begin with a list of questions to help guide Christians through the exploration process:

- **What do I like doing?** Our personal preferences do not always reflect God-given purpose, but sometimes they help us discern His calling.

- **What am I gifted at doing?** Early in my Christian walk, I tried several avenues of service to God. As I began to better understand my God-given gifts, I could become more focused in my service. Sometimes failure is simply part of the learning process.

- **What do others think I am good at doing?** I hate to say it, but even Christians can be delusional regarding their abilities. If I want to be a worship leader, but trusted leaders say I lack a sense of rhythm, I might want to reconsider my plans. Leaders do not always get it right, but wise input can also save us from a lot of embarrassment.

- **What types of service energize me?** This question has helped me considerably. Leading a small ministry requires me to perform many different tasks. By identifying which tasks energize and which ones drain, I can better focus the bulk of my effort.

- **What kinds of causes burden my heart?** Meaningful service to God often begins with a burden. Practically all I do in service to God began with a burden that developed during my mid-to-late twenties. So often, the Lord forms our hearts to align with His purposes for our lives.

- **What comes to mind if I daydream about serving others?** What God puts within us will seek to find expression, so it is wise to pay attention to our natural inclinations.

- **What do I believe the Lord has called me to do?** As much as all the previous questions matter, our King's will supersedes them all. And whatever the Lord calls us to do, He will empower us to do.

FULFILLING PURPOSE

Christ is the head of His body, and as we yield, He orchestrates the various parts and their movements. It is through this lens that we see both the beauty and wisdom of the church. Each local congregation has a distinct "flavor" that is influenced by the pastor and individual members. Together, local congregations then *complement* one another as they seek to meet needs and touch lives within their community and beyond.

The Lord continues to advance His kingdom through local congregations all over the globe, bringing freedom, life, and healing along the way. We can never forget that each individual has specific, God-given purposes, but no one ever stands alone. Always, we serve to complement the greater whole.

God calls pastors and leaders to help the members of the body work within the greater whole by encouraging, equipping, and empowering their people to accomplish His eternal purposes on earth. When this is done effectively, both the church and those around it experience the blessings of God. But when leaders fail to disciple, equip, and help people grow into their God-given purposes, everyone suffers.

I have seen priests, pastors, and leaders fail to fulfill their people-growing stewardship, with devastating results. Their congregations stay mired in apathy, thinking that dynamic service to God is limited only to the spiritual elite. Being the answer to every need might feed a pastor's ego, but it will destroy a community. With nothing to check their power, the forces of darkness wreak havoc on families and communities. But when church leaders grasp and effectively implement spiritual growth concepts, we see transformation on practically every level.

THE BOTTOM LINE

Spiritual maturity and Christian service go hand in hand. In this, pastors and leaders cannot force people to conform to their personal visions. Instead, we seek to reach and develop people to achieve their full potential as active members of the body of Christ.

Always, the church belongs to God, and as we yield to His Lordship, He will place and direct the various parts to accomplish His purposes on earth. Of course, individuals play vital roles, but only in conjunction with other parts of the body. Astute Christian leaders help facilitate this process, bringing salvation, healing, and transformation to many in need.

RELEVANT QUESTIONS

1. What is the connection between spiritual maturity and service to others?
2. What is the ultimate purpose of every church?
3. What is wrong with pastors "using" people to fulfill their personal visions?
4. What are some dangers of forcing people into roles that do not fit them well?
5. How can a leader help people find their places in the body of Christ?
6. When a person is used by God, how is his or her life affected?
7. How do Christians in a church complement one another?
8. How do churches in a community complement one another?
9. What happens to people when they lack a sense of purpose in the Lord?
10. What do you appreciate most about God's plan for His church?

CHAPTER TWENTY-EIGHT

EMPOWERING PEOPLE FOR CHANGE

Many people consider Jesus Christ to be one of the greatest, if not *the* greatest, teacher of morality to walk this earth. His teachings on love and humility left a mark on our planet that continues to this day. Unlike the era before Christ, when individuals, groups, and nations engaged in unjust actions, a global standard of morality now helps keep evil behavior from going entirely unchecked.

Of course, Jesus did not just teach about moral living, He also modeled it in a way that seemed extreme for His day. Among other things, Jesus did the following:

- Challenged unjust government and religious leaders
- Championed the cause of the downtrodden
- Treated women with honor and respect
- Consistently put the well-being of others above Himself
- Triumphed over greed in all its forms

In a world so often defined by warfare, Jesus Christ began a nonviolent revolution that eventually conquered the mighty Roman Empire. And while His moral teachings played a significant role in the process, a vital aspect of Jesus' methodology often goes unnoticed: *empowerment*.

THE DISCIPLES EMPOWERED

Not only did Jesus model ministry for His twelve disciples, He also sent them out as teams, empowering them for the challenging work ahead.

> Jesus summoned His twelve disciples and gave them authority over unclean spirits, to cast them out, and to heal every kind of disease and every kind of sickness. Matthew 10:1

Not content to limit His mission to the twelve, our Lord then commissioned seventy others for a similar quest. And while Luke 10 does not use the exact language of Matthew 10, the response of those seventy men reflects the power of God at work.

> The seventy returned with joy, saying, "Lord, even the demons are subject to us in Your name." And He said to them, "I was watching Satan fall from heaven like lightning. Behold, I have given you authority to tread on serpents and scorpions, and over all the power of the enemy, and nothing will injure you. Luke 10:17–19

While the Bible provides us with the names of Christ's twelve disciples, the Scriptures mention nothing about the identities of the seventy sent out by Jesus. These "nameless" men helped transform their nation by the authority of God and the anointing of the Holy Spirit. But the advancement of God's kingdom on earth was only just beginning!

THE CHURCH EMPOWERED

Church people tend to view successful ministry leaders as spiritually elite, and this is especially true of Jesus' apostles. We often laud the twelve (plus Paul) as uniquely spiritual individuals who are head and shoulders above the rest of humanity. But that perspective overlooks the fact that Jesus called twelve *ordinary* men (and one former persecutor) to launch His church.

Not only does elevating the apostles on a spiritual pedestal lack a core understanding of God's plan, it also provides a convenient excuse for lazy spirituality. After all, if we can never attain to their lofty standards, how can God expect us to even try? The Scriptures tell a different story, though.

> So when they had come together, they [the apostles] were asking Him, saying, "Lord, is it at this time You are restoring the kingdom to Israel?" He said to them, "It is not for you to know times or epochs which the Father has fixed by His own authority; but you will receive power when the Holy Spirit has come upon you; and you shall be My witnesses both in Jerusalem, and in all Judea and Samaria, and even to the remotest part of the earth." Acts 1:6–8

A large number of evangelical churches emphasize the *Great Commission* to make disciples of all nations, but how many embrace the empowerment of God's Spirit to accomplish the work? Without the empowering work of the Spirit, the quest to fulfill the Great Commission becomes yet another heavy burden laid upon the shoulders of devoted people. And the difference can be like that between using a handsaw and a chainsaw.

The advancement of God's kingdom on earth began with *one*—Jesus. Then it became *twelve*, and then *seventy*. On the Day of Pentecost, that number expanded to the *one hundred twenty* in the upper room. But then it spilled out into *thousands* on the street. And still, God was not finished.

> Now when they heard this, they were pierced to the heart, and said to Peter and the rest of the apostles, "Brethren, what shall we do?" Peter said to them, "Repent, and each of you be baptized in the name of

Jesus Christ for the forgiveness of your sins; and you will receive the gift of the Holy Spirit. For the promise is for you and your children and for all who are far off, as many as the Lord our God will call to Himself." Acts 2:37–39

Before long, God was doing miraculous works beyond the apostles through men such as Stephen (Acts 6:8). Even today, souls are being won to Christ in inhospitable nations as the Lord works through His people in miraculous ways.

HEALTHY LEADERSHIP

What would we think about a leader who routinely assigns tasks but never gives workers the resources needed to accomplish them? We would say he is a poor—and perhaps unjust—leader.

A friend's daughter once took a teaching job in a mid-Atlantic city several hours from home. After going through the difficulties of renting an apartment and moving her belongings, she began to prepare for the young students to arrive. Imagine her disappointment in discovering that the school had failed to provide the materials needed to teach the kids. It did not take someone with an education degree to recognize that the school was poorly run.

Our God is not an incompetent leader. Nor is He harsh like Pharaoh in demanding that slaves make bricks without straw. Whenever the Creator of our universe calls us to do something, we can be sure He will empower us to accomplish the task. The bigger question involves whether we are willing to embrace what God has to give.

Throughout the course of my life, I have seen considerable controversy regarding the work of the Holy Spirit. Without question, ego-driven people have wreaked all kinds of havoc in human lives. Unfortunately, those with weak character have become a convenient excuse to avoid the supernatural work of

God entirely. We can only begin to comprehend how the resulting lack of empowerment plays into the devil's hands.

Christian education serves a vital role; I encourage people to pursue it. But Bible school and seminary degrees do not a minister make. God also imparts oratory skills to communicate well and capture people's attention. But our Lord never limits Himself to using only the naturally gifted (1 Corinthians 1:26–29).

BEYOND OURSELVES

It has often been said that the Lord will never give us more than we can handle, but such a statement does not accurately reflect the Scriptures. Yes, with every temptation He provides a way of escape, but the Lord also has a habit of calling people to complete tasks beyond their natural abilities. In his second letter to the Corinthians, Paul wrote of being burdened excessively beyond strength so that he despaired even of life (2 Corinthians 1:8).

When it comes to serving God, we walk a fine line. Yes, service to the Lord should fit a person's temperament, gifts, and abilities. But because of the dangers of self-trust, elements of that service will require us to go beyond ourselves and our comfort zones. Discerning God's will becomes the primary issue because He always empowers His people to complete their assigned tasks.

Men such as Moses, Gideon, Elijah, and the twelve disciples provide relevant examples. Our efforts might not exactly replicate those of our forerunners in the faith, but they still require the empowerment of God's Spirit to be effective.

Our Creator loves to use people who are of no account in our world. This He does by empowering them through His Spirit. The idea is to minimize our temptation to boast by seeing the hand of God so obviously at work.

The Lord is not looking for the spiritually elite, but for those willing to believe His promises and lean into His grace. *Perhaps one of the most identifiable traits of a great man or woman of God involves a lifetime practice of drawing upon His sufficiency.* Serving well requires receiving well. And heaven remains ever ready to empower. The bigger question involves whether we draw upon that account.

THE ROLE OF THE LEADER

When it comes to empowerment, Christian leaders play a dual role. In a practical sense, they empower men and women to serve effectively by providing the opportunities and resources needed. And in a spiritual sense, they teach people how to lean into Christ's sufficiency.

All too often, though, leaders fear empowered church members. Some fears might have valid roots because of negative past experiences, while others are driven by insecurity and a quest to hold on to control.

Power in any form can be dangerous, and these ideas work effectively only when people are growing toward spiritual maturity. That is why Christian leaders must embrace a discipleship-growth mindset. The Bible's approach to ministry is *holistic*; God intends everything to work hand in hand. Only well-grounded believers can handle the exercise of spiritual power, and when we bypass vital issues related to character and spiritual growth, wineskins are bound to burst.

The secret to truly effective ministry involves not only empowering our people, but also helping them grow into the likeness of Jesus. When we wisely apply all the teachings of the Bible, no force in hell or on earth can stop the advancement of God's kingdom in our land.

THE BOTTOM LINE

A wise leader empowers people to help them accomplish the tasks they have been given, and our God is the ultimate leader. In order to protect hearts and display His glory, the Lord loves to use people who possess few natural gifts. So many of the heroes of our faith were simply ordinary people empowered by God. And the same God who used the ancients in mighty ways wants to do the same with us in these last days.

RELEVANT QUESTIONS

1. What happens when we embrace the moral teachings of Jesus but minimize the empowering work of His Spirit?
2. In what ways did Jesus empower His disciples to accomplish the work of the ministry?
3. What is significant about the progression from one, to twelve, to seventy, to one hundred twenty, and beyond?
4. Why do we err when we think that Christ's disciples were spiritually elite people?
5. Why does the Lord like to use people with few natural abilities?
6. Why do some leaders fear empowered people?
7. What happens when a leader fails to empower people for the tasks given to them?
8. What qualifies a person for ministry?
9. How do we draw upon Christ's sufficiency?
10. Why must empowered people be growing toward spiritual maturity?

CHAPTER TWENTY-NINE

REDEFINING SUCCESS

Jesus seemed to have little regard for diplomacy when relating to religious leaders. One day, as the Son of God taught about principles of stewardship, He offended a group of Pharisees by saying, "You are those who justify yourselves in the sight of men, but God knows your hearts; for that which is highly esteemed among men is detestable in the sight of God" (Luke 16:15b). Ouch!

The Greek word translated as "detestable" (*bdélugma*) in this verse hints of something with a foul, decaying odor[1]—an implication often related to idolatry in the Old Testament. What stands out even more, though, is the contrast. To think that God would be repulsed by something humanity applauds with envy! How can we be so blind to such a profound reality?

It should be no surprise that chaos prevails in so many areas of our globe. Natural human vision runs blind to our Creator's expectations and desires. And this is certainly true with the idea of *success*. Human goals and expectations—and especially the motives behind them—frequently conflict with heaven's design.

Humanity's concept of success is usually *quantitative*. We judge the value of our efforts by that which can be measured. Among a group of pastors, for example, success is often defined by the number of people who attend a church. But such a

---

1. Spiros Zodhiates, *The Complete Word Study Dictionary: New Testament* (Chattanooga, TN: AMG Publishers, 2000).

measurement might also be applied to a cult—which no godly pastor would describe as successful.

BEYOND NUMBERS

Numbers matter, of course, because they represent human souls. Even so, God's idea of success can differ greatly from ours. We get a taste of His expectations from the beginning of human history:

> Then God said, "Let Us make man in Our image, according to Our likeness; and let them rule over the fish of the sea and over the birds of the sky and over the cattle and over all the earth, and over every creeping thing that creeps on the earth." God created man in His own image, in the image of God He created him; male and female He created them. God blessed them; and God said to them, "Be fruitful and multiply, and fill the earth, and subdue it; and rule over the fish of the sea and over the birds of the sky and over every living thing that moves on the earth." Genesis 1:26–28

The very first words the Lord spoke to humanity were, "Be fruitful and multiply." We tend to think of fruitfulness in physical terms—as in having an abundance of children—but spiritual implications also apply.

While speaking of ancient Israel's great failure, the prophet Isaiah used some interesting words relating to fruitfulness:

> Let me sing now for my well-beloved
> A song of my beloved concerning His vineyard.
> My well-beloved had a vineyard on a fertile hill.
> He dug it all around, removed its stones,
> And planted it with the choicest vine.
> And He built a tower in the middle of it
> And also hewed out a wine vat in it;
> Then He expected it to produce good grapes,

> But it produced only worthless ones.
> "And now, O inhabitants of Jerusalem and men of Judah,
> Judge between Me and My vineyard.
> What more was there to do for My vineyard that I have not done in it?
> Why, when I expected it to produce good grapes did it produce worthless ones?
> So now let Me tell you what I am going to do to My vineyard:
> I will remove its hedge and it will be consumed;
> I will break down its wall and it will become trampled ground.
> I will lay it waste;
> It will not be pruned or hoed,
> But briars and thorns will come up.
> I will also charge the clouds to rain no rain on it."
>
> For the vineyard of the Lord of hosts is the house of Israel
> And the men of Judah His delightful plant.
> Thus He looked for justice, but behold, bloodshed;
> For righteousness, but behold, a cry of distress.
> Isaiah 5:1–7

In short, the nation of Israel was rejected for being unfruitful, or more specifically, for bearing bad fruit. But the fruit borne by Israel was not just bad; the Hebrew wording implicates it as worthless, stinking fruit marked by a stench.[2] The ancient Israelites bore no shortage of offspring, but their spiritual fruit stunk to high heaven.

Lest we think that the Israelites of Isaiah's era alone fell short of God's expectations, the Pharisees of the New Testament did no better. John the Baptist said to them:

> "You brood of vipers, who warned you to flee from the wrath to come? Therefore bear fruit in keeping with

---
2. Robert L. Thomas, *New American Standard Hebrew-Aramaic and Greek Dictionaries: Updated Edition* (Anaheim: Foundation Publications, Inc., 1998).

repentance; and do not suppose that you can say to yourselves, 'We have Abraham for our father'; for I say to you that from these stones God is able to raise up children to Abraham. The axe is already laid at the root of the trees; therefore every tree that does not bear good fruit is cut down and thrown into the fire."
Matthew 3:7b–10

Just a few years later, Jesus admonished a group that might have contained some of those very same Pharisees: "Therefore I say to you, the kingdom of God will be taken away from you and given to a people, producing the fruit of it" (Matthew 21:43). What a stinging rebuke to their prideful hearts!

GOD'S DEFINITION OF SUCCESS

Success, as defined by God, is not something we can achieve by natural ability or measure by human standards. Rather, it begins with sweet *spiritual fruit*—love, joy, peace, patience, kindness, goodness, faithfulness, gentleness, and self-control (see Galatians 5:22-23)—that is borne through an *abiding* relationship with God (John 15:1-8). *Fruitfulness is heaven's definition of success and a sign of spiritual maturity.*

Because spiritual fruit is the byproduct of a relationship with God, every person has the potential to bear the same quality of fruit. *Multiplication*, however, presents a different story. Whether good or bad, the fruit of our lives will be multiplied through various means such as relational connections, giftedness, hard work, and technology. We all have differing abilities and opportunities in this regard.

In no way am I suggesting that quantitative success is a bad thing—especially for churches. But when we have large numbers with minimal spiritual fruit, something is amiss. When the fruit of the Spirit is lacking, the fruit of the flesh—selfishness, haughtiness, and the quest for control—will abound. And this is why success in human eyes might be regarded as a colossal failure in God's.

It is in the realm of fruitfulness that we recognize the importance of drawing our sense of identity from a relationship with the Lord. Spiritual fruit abounds only as we serve from a place of security rather than attempting to draw our significance from visible success. Pride always kills spiritual fruit. *Fruitfulness is the expected product of spiritual life, finding its roots in a humble heart.* Indeed, humility is the fertilizer that causes spiritual fruit to grow sweet and bountiful.

The fruit of the Spirit is also *attractive*, inviting people to draw near and taste the sweetness of our Savior. Whether by showing kindness in a grocery store, interceding in a secret prayer closet, or humbly preaching from the pulpit of a church, we can never entirely grasp the influence we have on others. Certainly, the day will come when the fullness of our fruit is revealed for all to see. But for now, for today, we endeavor to humbly serve God and humanity, trusting Him for the desired results.

THE BOTTOM LINE

The Lord's ways are so much higher than ours. If we want to be successful in the eyes of heaven, we must redefine our understanding of success. From the beginning of time as we know it, God has always wanted us to bear the sweet fruit of the Spirit, and to multiply that fruit in the lives of those we serve.

RELEVANT QUESTIONS

1. In what ways do human goals and expectations often conflict with God's design?
2. Give some examples of things that might be highly esteemed by people but detested by God.
3. What is the danger of focusing on quantitative success in Christian ministry?

4. What does it mean to be fruitful?
5. What was the problem with the fruit borne by the ancient nation of Israel (Isaiah 5:1–7)?
6. What is heaven's definition of success?
7. What does the New Testament have to say about spiritual fruitfulness?
8. Why is it impossible for us to fully measure fruitfulness?
9. What role does humility play in living fruitfully?
10. Why is it necessary to draw our sense of identity from our relationship with God for our lives to be fully fruitful?
11. Why can we all bear the same quality of fruit but still have different levels of multiplication?
12. What are some means that can multiply the fruit of a person's life?

CHAPTER THIRTY

PERSEVERING THROUGH ADVERSITY

I have been around long enough to see more than a few sunsets—although I have not done nearly so well with sunrises! The passage of time has also brought many memories. People. Places. Experiences.

When I think about the people I have known throughout my decades of Christian experience, all kinds of thoughts flow through my mind. There are some who faithfully served the Lord, whose lifelong love for Christ never wavered, even as they approached death's door. Sadly, there have been others, including ministry leaders, who gave up on the faith and faded into spiritual oblivion.

Christian life and ministry can be far more difficult than expected, often causing people to lose heart and quit. They reason that if God is loving, true, and faithful, He will somehow spare them from extreme difficulty. Ironically, the Scriptures tell a different story.

EXPOSING THE MYTH

In the first chapter of his second letter to the Corinthians, the apostle Paul wrote about experiencing such adversity in ministry that he and his companions "despaired even of life" (2 Corinthians 1:8). In this passage, Paul exposes the "If God is in it, it must be easy" mentality for its deceptive nature. And yet, mysteriously, we continue to think that a life lived in devotion to the Lord will never be *really* hard. Perhaps it is because we do not grasp the apostle's perspective.

A little later in the epistle, Paul also penned the following:

> Therefore we do not lose heart, but though our outer man is decaying, yet our inner man is being renewed day by day. For momentary, light affliction is producing for us an eternal weight of glory far beyond all comparison, while we look not at the things which are seen, but at the things which are not seen; for the things which are seen are temporal, but the things which are not seen are eternal. 2 Corinthians 4:16–18

"Momentary, light affliction"—it does not sound like much, but remember, Paul had just written about despairing even of life. "Light affliction," in the apostle's mind, was not light in the sense of being easy to endure. Rather, Paul was comparing our earthly afflictions to the weight of glory we will experience in heaven. That wise apostle was viewing affliction through an eternal lens.

Some people say that God will never give us more than we can handle, but I think He routinely allows our lives to be challenged beyond our natural abilities. Sometimes, we bring the difficulties on ourselves, sometimes the devil attacks, and sometimes we must deal with the reality of a fallen planet. And it is not beyond reason for our adversities to be rooted in all three of these causes. Our Creator is not a sadist, but He endeavors to teach us to rely on Him instead of ourselves.

The danger of thinking that adversity will never be extreme is that we can begin to doubt God's goodness during the times we need to trust Him most. All too often, people lose heart and give up at the moment they need to buckle down and persevere. And the one failure worse than failing is quitting. Those who quit never fully mature because they do not allow God to write the end of their story. Spiritual maturity results from persevering when we want to give up. James reminds us:

> Consider it all joy, my brethren, when you encounter various trials, knowing that the testing of your faith produces endurance. And let endurance have its perfect result, so that you may be perfect and complete, lacking in nothing. James 1:2–4

Our world is full of prideful people who despise the authority of a sovereign God. So if we live as citizens and representatives of His kingdom, there will be those who treat us with disdain. To expect otherwise is to deceive ourselves.

Beyond dealing with self-centered men and women who oppose the Lord and His ways, we will also encounter a wide array of difficulties inherent to life on this fallen planet. Natural disasters, diseases, and miserable creatures such as ticks and mosquitoes can all turn our pursuit of the ideal life into an unpleasant struggle with reality.

Some might think that all the responsibility for blessing our lives belongs to God, but we also play a role in persevering and holding fast to the Lord—something Scripture encourages us to do time and time again. There is no boast in persevering; it is something we do only by the grace of God. And yet, the mysterious choice to endure belongs to us.

Returning to the Parable of the Sower, Jesus spoke of the seed that fell on rocky ground:

> "The one on whom seed was sown on the rocky places, this is the man who hears the word and immediately receives it with joy; yet he has no firm root in himself, but is only temporary, and when affliction or persecution arises because of the word, immediately he falls away." Matthew 13:20–21

The Lord also finished each of His seven letters to the Asian churches with a word of encouragement addressing the one "who overcomes" (Revelation 2:7, 11, 17, 26, and 3:5, 12, 21). And let us not forget how Jesus encouraged His followers to persevere in prayer:

> Now He was telling them a parable to show that at all times they ought to pray and not to lose heart. Luke 18:1

With multiple aspects of Christian living, and especially regarding prayer, we can identify an underlying theme that dictates the need for perseverance: unmet expectations. In far more circumstances than we can count, people lose heart and become discouraged because circumstances do not work out as they expect. This, of course, is no fault of God's.

ENCOURAGEMENT TO PERSEVERE

The Lord is ever faithful and always true to His promises. But He works in ways unlike ours, and on a timetable of His own choosing. Unfortunately, from our limited perspective, we often consider prayers delayed to be prayers unanswered.

It is also common for Christians to lose heart when they feel they have invalidated God's promises because of a personal failure—as though that stopped Him from using flawed people such as Abraham, Moses, David, Peter, and Paul.

Others might struggle with the nagging sense that their service to God is not accomplishing much. But the dynamics of spiritual growth can be challenging to gauge. Sometimes, invisible roots are growing deeper. At other times, circumstances are building to a tipping point. The bottom line is that God can be doing a powerful work outside our limited field of view. And these apparently fruitless seasons can last for what seems to be a lifetime. I cannot help but wonder how many people give up on faith at a time when they should be pressing into His promises.

Regardless of the reason for discouragement, we each play a vital role as we encourage and exhort one another to endure hardship and persevere for the glory of God. The writer of Hebrews stated it well:

> Take care, brethren, that there not be in any one of you an evil, unbelieving heart that falls away from the living God. But encourage one another day after day, as long as it is still called "Today," so that none of you will be hardened by the deceitfulness of sin. For we have become partakers of Christ, if we hold fast the beginning of our assurance firm until the end. Hebrews 3:12–14

Sometimes—especially during discouraging seasons—days feel as though they last forever. But when we step back to survey the big picture, we realize how quickly life on this earth passes. What feels like long suffering will soon bear its sweet fruit, and it is then that everything begins to come into perspective.

> Blessed is the man who remains steadfast under trial, for when he has stood the test he will receive the crown of life, which God has promised to those who love him. James 1:12 (ESV)

THE BOTTOM LINE

Life rarely goes as we expect, and growing to maturity requires that we trust God's promises and endure hardship during the dark seasons of life. The Lord reigns over our universe and holds all things in the palm of His hand. He never fails to move when the time is right, but we must endure, continuing to trust even when His plans do not meet our expectations. Encouraging one another to persevere in the faith is one of the most powerful things we can do.

RELEVANT QUESTIONS

1. Why do people mistakenly think that faithful servants of God will never experience extreme difficulty?
2. What Scriptures can you identify that challenge those false assumptions?
3. According to James 1:2–4, what is the connection between adversity and spiritual maturity?
4. What are some reasons that life can be really hard for a Christian in this world?
5. What are some primary reasons Christians lose heart?
6. Why does it often feel as though our service to God is in vain, or that our prayers are falling on deaf ears?
7. Identify some Bible verses that encourage believers to faithfully persist.
8. Can you recall a season of adversity when another person's encouragement kept you from giving up?
9. What makes encouragement so powerful?
10. What are some ways in which we can encourage one another to persevere?

ACKNOWLEDGMENTS

I consider it a great honor to write books related to Christian growth and am deeply appreciative of the faithful servants of God who help make it happen.

In the case of *The Teleios Trail*, I want to extend my deep appreciation to Kevin Bordeaux, Deb Croyle, Scott Dalton, K-Lee Gaffney, Dave Herndon, Jason Hutchins, Jackie Kuehn, Lynda Logue, Samantha Mitchell, Elaine Rice, Joe Ryer, Debi Santos, Paula Saylor, Todd Stanley, Mark Sterlace, and Judah Thomas for their wonderful contributions to this challenging but vital project.

I like to say that we all do our part when it comes to advancing God's kingdom, and their part has proven invaluable to me.

ADDITIONAL RESOURCES FROM SEARCH FOR ME MINISTRIES

Paperback copies of *The Teleios Trail: Thirty Topics to Explore for Spiritual Growth* can be purchased through major online retailers. Volume discounts are available through SfMe Ministries (sfme.org) for ministry organizations.

Division has long plagued the church, reflecting badly on Christianity and hindering our mission. **Greater Glory: The Transformational Power of Christian Unity** challenges us to embrace God's perspective so we can live out the lifestyle of love that is central to our faith. (Audiobook available)

There is a profound logic behind all that God does, but it is not human logic. **The Age of Abiding: Experiencing the Life of the Vine** provides powerful insights into human nature, helping the reader better grasp the mysterious beauty of the Christian gospel. (Audiobook available)

The Search for Rest: Fifty Days to a More Peaceful Life provides an awesome personal or group study that explores the concept of the Sabbath from both spiritual and physical perspectives. This thought-provoking book meets a powerful need in a world that is filled with anxiety and unrest. (Audiobook available)

Much of the Christian faith makes little sense to the modern, Western mind because the Bible was written with a mentality that differs from current thought. **Drinking Truth: Embracing the Covenant Mindset of the Bible** provides an insightful look at the new covenant in light of the covenantal mindset with which the Bible was penned. (Audiobook available)

The **Community Prayer Devotional** is a powerful book that brings churches together to pray. Even better, the cover can be personalized to fit your community, allowing people to take ownership and embrace prayer as a lifestyle! (Audiobook available)

If you want to gain a Biblical perspective on identity, ***From Glory to Glory: Finding Real Significance in an Image-Driven World*** is the book for you! Not only is this powerful forty-day devotional filled with illuminating insights, it will also help to renew your mind as a beloved child of the King of Glory. (Audiobook available)

Say Goodbye to Regret: Discovering the Secret to a Blessed Life is a life-changing book that deals with the problem of regret on two fronts. Learn how to move beyond the lingering pain of regret and also how to avoid regrets entirely by pursuing the rich treasures of God's spiritual wisdom. (Audiobook available)

The TouchPoint: Connecting with God through the Bible is a valuable resource for those who are interested in learning more about the Bible. Revised in 2020, this book provides a great introduction to the Christian Scriptures while emphasizing a personal relationship with God. (Audiobook available)

The Divine Progression of Grace: Blazing a Trail to Fruitful Living thoughtfully explores God's grace from a perspective of empowerment as well as acceptance. This book will take you deeper into a relationship with your Creator and also help make you more usable for His purposes.

Each reading in ***Champions in the Wilderness: Fifty-Two Devotions to Guide and Strengthen Emerging Overcomers*** draws from a deep well of truth to encourage, strengthen, and instruct those who desire to walk with God but are struggling in the face of adversity. The format of this devotional lends itself well to group discussion. (Audiobook available)

ABOUT THE AUTHOR

Bob Santos writes to see lives transformed by God's goodness. Years of working in college ministry revealed that people crave to know more about God not only in their hearts through faith, but also through a deeper understanding of the truths found in His Word.

Pursuing spiritual vitality, Bob helps others "connect the dots" of Biblical truth by addressing "missing links" of contemporary theology. In this, Bob's books and video teachings explore key Biblical themes—such as covenants, grace, identity, rest, unity, and wisdom—that are often misunderstood or widely ignored. His explanations of difficult concepts, combined with inspirational messages of hope in Christ, are insightful, thought-provoking, and transformational as they explore the Christian faith in an understandable and yet intellectually satisfying way.

Bob was licensed for Christian ministry in 1997 and ordained in 2005 through Elim Fellowship (www.elimfellowship.org). In 2006, Bob and his wife Debi founded Search for Me Ministries, Inc. (sfme.org) with the mission to help form and equip a generation of world changers for Christ through the production of Biblically-based teaching resources.

College sweethearts, Bob and Debi have been married for over forty years. Together, they have two adult children, two grandchildren, and three granddogs. When he is not writing, speaking, or leading a Bible study, you will likely find Bob doing something in the great outdoors.

POSTING BOOK REVIEWS

Please consider posting an online review of this book. Honest reviews are deeply appreciated and provide an easy way for our readers to contribute to our ministry efforts. Also, if your life has been touched by one of our resources, please recommend it to others.

SFME MEDIA

SfMe Media belongs to Search for Me Ministries, Inc. (SfMe Ministries)—an IRS-recognized 501(c)(3) nonprofit organization. Search for Me Ministries burns with a vision to help form and equip a generation of world changers for Christ. We believe in the importance of reaching those who do not know the Lord, but we also recognize the need for healthy churches as landing places for new believers. By helping Christians grow to maturity with our uniquely flavored teaching resources, we are helping to create environments that foster the fulfillment of the Great Commission in every way.

www.ingramcontent.com/pod-product-compliance
Lightning Source LLC
Chambersburg PA
CBHW070135080526
44586CB00015B/1702